being different

Lambda Youth Speaks Out

being different

Lambda Youths Speak Out

By Larry Dane Brimner

The Lesbian and Gay Experience

FRANKLIN WATTS
A Division of Grolier Publishing
New York / London / Hong Kong / Sydney
Danbury, Connecticut

Library of Congress Cataloging-in-Publication Data

Brimner, Larry Dane.
Being different : lambda youths speak out / by Larry Dane Brimner.
p. cm. — (The lesbian and gay experience)
Includes bibliographical references and index.
Summary: Gay and lesbian teenagers relate their experiences regard-
ing the discovery and acceptance of their sexual orientation.
ISBN 0-531-11222-5 (library binding)
ISBN 0-531-15188-3 (trade)
ISBN 0-531-15758-x
1. Gay teenagers—North America—Social conditions—Juvenile litera-
ture. 2. Lesbian teenagers—North America—Social conditions—Juvenile
literature. 3. Coming out (Sexual orientation)—North America—Juvenile
literature. [1. Homosexuality. 2. Gays—Identity. 3. Lesbians—Identity. 4.
Coming out (Sexual orientation)] I. Title. II. Series.
HQ76.3.N67B75 1995   95-7679
305.23'5—dc20   CIP
                               AC

contents

5

To lambda youths
everywhere—
know that there is a
rainbow.

acknowledgments

As always, there are many people to thank for helping to make a book a reality.

I am indebted to my wise editor and friend, E. Russell Primm III, for suggesting the book to me in the first place, for shuttling crates of helpful clippings my way, for making me laugh when the grim statistics seemed overwhelming, for making framework and editorial suggestions, and for giving me great creative freedom.

I am also indebted to John Selfridge and Franklin Watts for having the courage to undertake this topic.

I am grateful to my "group," the writer friends with whom I meet once a month. They are Sheila Cole, Jean Ferris, and Kathleen Krull. These talented folks provided much-needed moral support, more clippings, and lightened things up when threats came my way.

I am equally grateful to Dr. Helen Foster James, Dr. Paul Erickson, Tim Lowry, John Kendryna, Joe Hosking, Jessea Greenman, Deacon Maccubbin, Ekem Merchant, Robert Riddle, Jill Pollack, Tom Jevec, Kevin Boyer, Doug Kehoe, Sandy Miller, The Gerber/Hart Library and Archives, The Center—San Diego, Gay

Youth Alliance—San Diego, the Obelisk Bookstore, Lambda Rising Bookstore, Alyson Publications, Project 21, Horizons, the Universal Fellowship of Metropolitan Community Churches, and the AIDS Foundation of San Diego for keeping me abreast of current information and for yet more clippings.

I thank Jim for being my first reader.

Finally, I thank the courageous young people who contacted me with a willingness to share their personal stories and thoughts about being different. They are Anthony R. Ashley, Bonnie Margay Burke, Melanie-Joy Cohn, Trey Harris, Christopher, Curtis, Dan, David, Eric, Rica, Shawn, Scott, Shulamit, Susan, and Terra. Their words will have the greatest impact on the other young lesbian and gay people who will read this book.

The honest personal story is the most powerful message. Whether in the form of poetry or video or AA testimonial, the first-person story has the power to move emotions, open minds, touch hearts, and burst barriers in a way that no other human statement can do.

The personal stories of gay youth are doubly powerful, because they shatter the very foundation of prejudice and preconceived notions. While I was working as a volunteer teacher at EAGLES Center in Los Angeles, the fundamentalist preacher Lou Sheldon had to confront several of our high-school students on a southern California radio talk-show. Our kids boldly went head to head with this behemoth of conservatism. They didn't give him an inch. So compelling were their personal stories, and their heartfelt statements, that the fire-and-brimstone-breathing Sheldon was shaken.

"I had a hard time with this," he confessed afterwards," according to one teacher that was there. "Those kids reminded me of my own grandchildren."

"My own" is ultimately what stories from gay kids are about. Religious extremists would have us believe that creating a highly controlled family environment is the one sure way to avoid having homosexual children. Not so. Gay, lesbian, bisexual, transvestite, and transgender children crop up in the most religious and loving families. Ultimately, the enemy of homosexuality has one chance in ten of finding himself warring against his own flesh and blood. A retired naval officer I know, who was violently opposed to allowing gays in the military, found to his shock that his own daughter and his own favorite niece were both lesbians. In fact, his daughter was serving in uniform. As a loving father, he was forced to temper his views.

Indeed, in the larger family of humans, we are all injured by the guilt, terror, and deviousness that are fostered in our children as a result of extremist efforts to keep homosexuality criminalized.

Open statements by gay kids have the power to sway voters. When gay students stepped to the mike during a spring 1995 Los Angeles Board of Education meeting, they spoke out against attempts by the Christian Coalition to influence the school election and scuttle all gay-friendly programs in the progressive L.A. Unified district. The televised board meetings are widely watched in the Southland, because of the volatile nature of the L.A. social scene. Despite public apathy toward the election, gay board member Jeff Horton was re-elected by a resounding 61 percent of the vote. The kids' stories had been heard.

Straight adults who can dismiss heart-rending tales of adult coming-out, even adult death from AIDS, have a hard time blowing off the same kind of story from a teenager. The very idea of a fourteen-year-old boy being thrown out on the street because of his sexual belief, of a sixteen-year-old girl suffering assault and battery by her parents because of being lesbian, goes against the grain of what we all know should be society's protection of youth. No society can afford to discard its gay young as so much garbage.

Today, gay youth are coming out younger, in greater numbers, than in the '60s and '70s. My youngest students at EAGLES Center were thirteen—battle-scarred veterans of social war in junior high. They were sure of their sexual orientation. The only question in their minds was how they would survive. These kids make an awesomely adult decision at the age of thirteen, fifteen, eighteen. Most nongay adults never in their lives make such a life-and-death decision, requiring such courage in the face of so little support and such overwhelming social odds, risking assault at home from hostile relatives, as well as bashing at school.

Yet these direct assaults on their persons and their personas are not the only problem that gay youth have.

They face a broader dilemma: American youth in general are seen but not heard. Yes, our culture is obsessively fixated on looking young. Yes, youth's spendable income is courted by the media, the fashion industry, and other big business. But all this supposed influence comes handcuffed by disenfranchisement. Young people under eighteen can't vote. Today, as the country tightens up, they have diminishing legal standing to demand free speech and other human rights. Censorship of school publications, corporal punishment in schools, the "right" of parents to control and proselytize and pressure a child, even the forcible institutionalization of a maverick or suicidal kid "for his own good," is currently being stepped up. So kids must rely on adult lobbies, advocacy groups, sympathetic juvenile judges, and the media in order to be heard.

With nongay minors expected to live in such powerlessness, it is no wonder that gay kids have a hard time getting their stories in print.

Today, more and more young people lash out at their own powerlessness at a young age. Often their acts of defiance harm others, and themselves: the decisions to have sex, flout custody, run away from home, do drugs or alcohol or graffiti, have a baby out of wedlock, work as a prostitute, risk exposure to AIDS, strew violence, injure or kill another person — even kill themselves. Nor are these decisions being limited to youth from decaying urban ghettos—they are also made by kids from well-off families. Hard times and joblessness are driving more and more young people to get money by illegal means.

Amidst all the current efforts to "get tough on kids," few people are heeding the clear message being sent by youth. May I suggest that any society that seeks to get respect by coercion and at gunpoint will not get it. Women whose human rights are violated do secretly despise the men who seek to control them by force. Blacks, Latinos, Native Americans, Asians have never respected white racist gunpoint. Catholics and Protestants have not respected each other's historic coercions. Today our youth—including gay youth—are showing contempt for authorities who demand respect at gunpoint, yet who deny them any real power, or voice.

Paradoxically, our society does turn around and admit that a minor is capable of making a positive, intelligent, and informed decision—like falling in love with the right person, getting married, joining the military. A judge with a heart will allow a minor to question what parent he or she wants to live with. Young kids can have a clear vision of their career dreams, too. Who among us hasn't known a boy who wanted to be a cop at age thirteen, or a girl who wanted to be a lawyer at fifteen? I wanted to be a writer at age ten, and never wavered from this dream in fifty years!

Society even applauds and honors a minor's move into religion—whether a thirteen-year-old Jewish girl's decision to celebrate her Bat Mitzvah, or a Native American child's decision to seek the first vision quest.

Indeed, history recognizes that a teenager has the power to topple governments and move armies into battle—as did Joan of Arc.

In the face of so much evidence that kids are capable of sound decisions, why do so many people continue to deny that young people have the power, and the right, to make decisions and statements about their sexual orientation?

Again and again, I have seen the power of young people's stories to step beyond marches and rhetoric—to move us and shame us and inspire us, and make us see the starkness of commonplace in their lives.

Today, our new gay youth tell their stories in a time when issues of gay life are publicly debated, as they were not during my teenage years. Today, young gay people are fighting to keep not merely the victories that gay rights have already won, but their very lives. As a price for their openness, they face stepped-up brutality, joblessness, homelessness, seizure of their children by the state. Indeed, they will face long prison terms—if religious lobbyists and legislators who want to stiffen sodomy laws have their way with the American voter.

In the following pages, author Larry Brimner lets us hear these young voices—silenced so long behind the black curtain of disenfranchisement. These are the stories that would be blue-penciled out of most school publications.

—Patricia Nell Warren
author of *The Front Runner*
Los Angeles, May 1995

introduction

Not long ago I received a letter in reaction to an earlier book of mine about the internment of Japanese Americans called *Voices from the Camps*, and the author of that letter called me a "liberal commie" because, I assume, he felt the suspension of constitutional rights that I discussed in that book was justified given the time and situation. His label amused me, though, because those who know me well would say that I'm about as conservative as a person gets. I was raised with a solid foundation in the work ethic. I was taught to respect others, regardless of age, and hold that we all have a duty—even highly paid sports personalities who claim exemption—to be positive role models for those younger than ourselves. I try to walk through life as quietly as possible, hoping that my actions don't cause others discomfort. For this reason, I'm cautious with my public language, as words are powerful and can be injurious; they have pained me. This is hardly the textbook description of a *liberal*.

Yet, I also have a firm belief in fairness. I believe men and women who do the same job deserve the same compensation. I believe that a democratic government has a responsibility to guarantee equal treatment of *all* people. I believe that the freedom of speech does not include the right to silence others. And although I was given a solid spiritual foundation early in life, I have never felt it within my rights to force my religious beliefs and practices on others. I now count among my friends Catholics, Jews, Protestants, Buddhists, and even atheists, and their differences are partly why I value them as friends. They add richness to my life. If these views make me a liberal, then so I am.

Obviously, I'm difficult to pigeonhole, as are most people. Labels don't serve much purpose unless they are narrowly applied. A person may be liberal in one area and quite conservative in another. But there is one label that universally stirs emotions and often draws quick condemnation: homosexual. One researcher states that "[h]omosexuals are arguably the most hated group of people in the United States."[1]

Because it is based on myths and hearsay, the emnity directed at homosexuals is irrational. Moreover, these misinformed impressions are extended to an entire group. When this happens, it forms biases and is called *prejudice*. Time was when biases and prejudices formed the descriptions of African-Americans and Hispanics. "They're all good dancers" or "They're all lazy" were common stereotypes used to describe these two groups of people. Only when individual African-Americans marched for equality and when Cesar Chavez brought focus to the back-breaking work done by individual Hispanic laborers were those false images shaken—*shaken* as opposed to *destroyed*, because old myths always lurk in the darkness of ignorance and threaten to replace truth. The fact is that most people don't know any homosexuals, or are not aware of the sexual orientation of those they do know. Their opinions have been formed in ignorance.

When my editor asked me to do a book about lesbian and gay teenagers, I knew it would be a controversial step, given the current conservative bent of society, and admittedly, I hedged, asking for a few days to think it over. I was already an established children's picture book and middle-grade nonfiction author. I knew that Nancy Garden had come under pressure for writing *Annie on My Mind*. Marion Dane Bauer's involvement with *Am I Blue? Coming Out From Silence* cost her a speaking engagement. Simply put, I wasn't certain that I was up to having to defend a book of my own.

I also knew that doing a book about and for lesbian and gay teens would open some old and very personal wounds.

While weighing the pros and cons of the proposed book, I made a trip to the South to fulfill a speaking engagement. Because I often speak at reading conferences and schools about the writing process, there was nothing unusual about the trip—until I went to dinner with a small group of elementary school librarians. During the course of the evening, one librarian asked, "What are you working on now?" Naively, I answered, "I'm considering a book about lesbian and gay teens." The sudden silence at the table was deafening, the kind that signals a major *faux pas*. When the librarian recovered, she drew herself up and said, "I'm born-again. If you write a book on *that* topic, I'll see to it that you never sell another picture book in my school system." At that point, I didn't know what to say, and the evening stumbled forward with my conversational contributions limited to a few *yes*es, *no*s, and *how nice*s.

As uncomfortable as that evening was, I'm glad I was there because it forced me to think about my own search for sexual identity when I was an adolescent and the dearth of materials greeting that search. The first time I knowingly heard the word *homosexual* was when David, a high-school friend, said to me one day, "I think I'm a homosexual." I knew from the sound of his voice that a homosexual, whatever it was, wasn't something he wanted to be, so I said, "No way. You can't be that." Mind you, I didn't draw a connection between *queer*, which I heard often in the hallways at school, and *homosexual*. My big brother had explained what a *queer* was when I was about seven or eight: "A queer is a person who sits in the bathtub and watches the bubbles his farts make." In high school, I had learned another definition: A queer wears green on Thursdays. In my rural and somewhat isolated youth, *queer* didn't have a sexual connotation; and as far as I knew, it had never been directed at me. After all, I never wore green on Thursdays and always took showers.

It wasn't until I was in college that I came to a limited understanding of homosexuality and the sexual connotation of *queer,* and I was terrified to think that these terms might have significance to my own life. In college, I became acutely aware—as opposed to the *vague* awareness I had when I was four or five—of my attraction to other men. Although I always had girlfriends, my eyes and mind wandered when I was with them, and it wasn't long until I was visiting the library to look up *homosexuality*. Unlike my high-school library, the university library had books on the topic, but they were "Desk Reserve." This meant they had to be requested at the desk—and there was no way I was going to do that. Hence, my reading was limited to case studies in textbooks that were assigned in psychology classes, and I never seemed to fit any of the descriptions I encountered there, except for the general one—a same-sex attraction. Certainly, I wasn't suicidal, I didn't prey on children, and my family was only as neurotic as the one next door.

What followed was a long period of denial. When my parents finally became suspicious and confronted me, they let me know in very clear terms that if I was *that way*, I could forget about support. To hammer home the point, my mother said I could forget about a teaching career as well; she would see to it that I never stepped foot in a classroom. My dad took to calling me "Laura," on the few occasions when he spoke to me at all; he said if I wanted to *fix* myself I should get psychiatric help. I didn't want to disappoint my parents. I was a good son, so I was willing to do anything they said. The ensuing months were a blur of psychiatric appointments, electroshock treatments, arguments, and tears that ultimately led to two suicide attempts.

Until that dinner with the born-again librarian, those memories had lain deep within my mind. But that evening I was also jolted into recalling the difficulty I had grappling with my own sexuality while, at the same time, trying to obtain a teaching job. I graduated with honors and was named "Outstanding Student Teacher of the Year," but it meant little to school personnel officers, not if they suspected an applicant might be homosexual. This became clear to me when I interviewed with an Escondido, California, school system and was told that they didn't hire homosexuals. Ironically, they discovered one on staff the very next year—a college classmate of mine who had slipped through their screening process—and they immediately demanded and got his resignation.

Eventually, a teaching job did materialize, and I proved myself. A better teaching job opened up the next year, and I got that. Several school systems later, I found myself teaching in El Centro, California, but I was still in denial about my sexuality. But some of the gay students at the high school sensed a kinship and one, a senior named Aurelio, asked if we could "see" each other. Another, Jose, told me that he hated himself because of the feelings he was having. He never mentioned that they were homosexual feelings. He didn't have to. I was poorly prepared to offer them advice or even to be a role model, so I shunned them both. It was easier at the time than dealing with what I was denying.

When I recalled these events and others—the school superintendent, with whom I roomed for a while, who hid his own homosexuality behind the cover of a wife and two children and who suggested I do the same if I wanted to be successful; the "straight" school board member who demanded lunch-time sex in exchange for not recommending my dismissal; the father of a student and president of our school's booster club who wanted to "fool around" on evenings when his wife was busy; and another suicide attempt—I grew sad and angry. Those painful events were all a long time ago. In the interim, I had gone on to become a college instructor and, after that, a full-time writer, lecturer, and writing consultant to school systems nationwide. I had come to appreciate my own sexual orientation, established a nurturing relationship, one that has endured seventeen years, and reunited bonds with my family. But I was sad and angry just the same.

I came home from the South and told my editor that I would do the book because young lesbians and gays should not be denied role models or accurate, straightforward information about their sexuality. They shouldn't have to hide who they are, nor should poorly formed societal attitudes put them in a position where suicide becomes their only avenue of hope. Their dignity and pride should not be chipped away one chink at a time.

Doing this book has been one of the most interesting adventures of my life. I met some bright, talented young people who are determined to make a difference in this world. You'll read their stories. I was forced to become more computer adept, because the younger generation transits the electronic highway with much agility. Many of their contributions arrived over my modem. I received a threat in the mail from a religious conservative in Asheville, North Carolina, who warned that "There is no fire escape in hell." A fellow writer dropped me from her circle of friends because she felt the topic of my book was unsavory, but others stepped up to prove their friendship by offering encouragement and information— enough for two books!

I will be mightily surprised if this book is not challenged by someone, somewhere. From its first inception, there have been hints that the road might be bumpy. So be it. But let me remind you of something that Dwight D. Eisenhower once said, "Don't think you are going to conceal thoughts by concealing evidence that they ever existed." Looking through a list of books challenged or banned in 1992 and 1993, I saw a recurring trend: Books with lesbian and gay themes appeared again and again. Repeatedly, critics claimed that such books "promote a dangerous and ungodly lifestyle from which children must be protected" or that they indoctrinate children "into the gay lifestyle." In every school, in every city, in every state, in every country, there are sexual-minority youths who are wishing desperately to find themselves portrayed in books. Excising books with lesbian and gay themes from school and public libraries will not make sexual-minority youths disappear.

Let me say now that this book is neither meant to promote, nor to indoctrinate. It was written solely to acknowledge that lesbian and gay teenagers exist everywhere, to answer their questions by providing them with current information and alternate, frequently silenced viewpoints, and to give them some comfort; if there is a crossover to other reading audiences, I hope it gives cause for thought and dialogue—nothing more.

If it comforts even one at-risk teenager, then it will have been worth the journey.

A NOTE ON TERMINOLOGY

Throughout this book I have used the terms *homosexual*, *sexual-minority youth*, *lesbian* (for female), and *gay* (for male). In no way should readers draw the conclusion that by using these terms I am excluding *bisexual*, *transgendered*, and *transsexual* youths. This book is meant to be inclusive even when the specific terminology has been omitted.

Larry Dane Brimner
San Diego, California
1995

on being different

An unprecedented number of young people are acknowledging their homosexuality and publicly accepting it as natural, without any of the judgments that society often places upon it. Yet, they live in a world biased toward heterosexuality and one which is fraught with myths, ignorance, and misinformation about "the sex that dare not speak its name," as Oscar Wilde called *homosexuality*. That they reach any level of self-acceptance is no small achievement.

For many teens, adolescence is a difficult and confusing time, and they may or may not have individuals with whom they can discuss issues of sexuality and receive factual information. Their parents may feel uncomfortable with the topic, or worse, not be able to provide *accurate* information. Their schools may offer little more. While some schools should be praised for their factual and even-handed sex-education programs, others have been hampered by inadequate funding, opposition from conservative forces in the community, poorly trained faculty, or a combination of these things. When it comes down to it, far too many teens learn about sex and sexuality—for better or worse, correctly or incorrectly—from the mass media and/or their peers.

For homosexual teens—*lesbians* and *gays*—the difficulties and confusions surrounding adolescence are often compounded. Most of the relationships they have read about in books and periodicals and viewed on television and in films have been heterosexual—*straight*. As one researcher stated, "The *implicit* message sent to gay youth by the media is 'you do not exist.'"[1] When the media does acknowledge their existence, the image of homosexuality it sends is usually distorted and spurious.

In American society, heterosexuality is largely taken for granted. Young people live in a world that assumes them to be heterosexual. Indeed, the two organizations that have the strongest and most long-lasting impact on them—families and schools—usually make this blanket assumption.[2] In essence, the result is that heterosexual youth have been "trained," as it were, from the outset of life to step into predictable sexual roles, while young lesbians and gays typically are left adrift.

Even so, most lesbian and gay youths say they felt somehow different from their straight peers at a very early age, but they had nothing in their experience to explain what that difference was. Later—most typically between the ages of twelve and fourteen—when they realize that this *difference* is an attraction to persons of their own sex, or *homosexual* feelings, they have only society's whispered myths with which to identify.[3]

Those myths tell lesbian and gay teens that "they are criminals, sinners, or mentally ill."[4] As evil and destructive as these myths are, they persist because homosexuality has been largely invisible in American society. Historically, only the most extreme and sensational elements of homosexual behavior were reported. These images, these stereotypes, became the standard by which *all* lesbian and gay people were judged. And it continues. The stereotypes give credence to the erroneous images held by the uninformed. Young lesbians and gays, on the other hand, are left feeling "unnatural, abnormal, and despised."[5] These are the feelings that become their self-definition, in spite of personal histories that usually contradict such negative images. This is the disparity between society's and religion's depiction of homosexuals and the reality of who these young people are. Yet, because society and religions have said that homosexuality is bad, many young lesbians and gays, upon acknowledging their same-sex attraction, begin to believe that they, too, are bad.

To avoid the negative associations of being labeled homosexual, they sometimes invent boyfriends or girlfriends whom friends and family never quite meet. They take fictitious field trips to museums and spend long hours at the library "studying" in order to explain their absences when they attend meetings of gay youth or become involved in a relationship. But leading a double life can take its toll. Aside from the guilt that lying brings about, some youths develop substance abuse problems. One study cited that 58 percent of the young gay males interviewed had some kind of problem with drugs, alcohol, or both.[6] Many run away rather than deal with the repercussions of being "found out" by family and friends. Lesbian and gay youths account for approximately one-quarter of all the homeless youth in the United States.[7]

Other sexual-minority youths try to hide their true feelings and "pass" as heterosexuals in other ways. To compensate for their homosexual feelings and to avoid being called "faggot" or "dyke" by their peers, they often boastfully and frequently engage in relations with the opposite sex.[8] But hiding one's true feelings and passing as heterosexual when one is not is injurious to an individual's emotional well-being. What these young people experience is similar to the psychological damage endured by Jews who passed as Christians in Nazi Germany, or by blacks who passed as white in the old South.[9]

There is also the widely shared and false notion that if homosexual feelings are denied long enough, they will simply disappear. While denial will not make those same-sex attractions vanish, it will succeed in destroying the self-esteem and integrity of lesbian and gay youths. And with this, denial will also bring isolation induced by a fear of becoming outcast by their family, friends, religion, and—according to one Canadian study—even their ethnic group.[10]

Isolation breeds its own devastation. The Bush Administration's Department of Health and Human Services reported that 30 percent of all teenage suicides were gay related. In numbers, this translates to a staggering 1,500 young lesbian and gay deaths every year in the United States.[11] For many sexual-minority youths, suicide becomes a means of coping with being different. Twenty-year-old Bobby Griffith was one who saw suicide as a viable way of dealing with same-sex attraction. Feeling isolated and lacking support from his family, friends, and high school, he jumped from a freeway overpass into the path of an eighteen-wheeler and was killed instantly. At sixteen, he had written in his diary: "I can't let anyone find out that I'm not straight. . . . My friends would hate me, I just know it. They might even want to beat me up. And my family? . . . They've said they hate gays, and even God hates gays, too. It really scares me now, when I hear my family talk that way, because now, they are talking about me. . . . Sometimes I feel like disappearing from the face of this earth."[12]

Sadly, feelings of depression, self-loathing, and self-destruction are commonplace among lesbian and gay youths when they are faced daily with heterosexual images, and especially when positive homosexual images are denied them. One study indicated that "about a third" of young, self-labeled lesbians and gays had in the past attempted suicide.[13]

Nothing puts a "face" on lesbian and gay teenagers and their inner turmoil better than the youths themselves. Three young people speak out about their struggles with dignity in the accounts that follow.

MELANIE-JOY, 19, Coral Springs, Florida

Expectations

hide it all
inside yourself
don't let out
your feelings
give lots of hugs,
lots of smiles
laugh a lot
people like that

as you grow up
don't let them know
all the feelings
you harbor inside
a walking-time-bomb
suicide is love
death is friend

BONNIE, 21, San Diego, California

My first sexual memory was walking into my parents' bedroom while they were busy procreating. Later, I recall seeing my mother having sex with another woman. I had no preconceived notions about sexuality. Both situations were confusing and scary to me. Because my parents never dis-

cussed anything sexual with my two brothers, my sister, or myself, I was not given the luxury of an explanation of either encounter.

As a Roman Catholic, I was trained to be obedient and to never question my elders. I feel that this kind of rearing, along with a complete lack of communication in my household, set me up to be a victim of sexual abuse for much of my childhood. My father's best friend came over every Saturday and molested me and my little brother for years.

I anesthetized my pain early on with food, overeating to fill up the raw emptiness inside of me and to hide in my obesity. After the abuse stopped, I found that not eating helped me to feel more in control of my body—a neurotic reclaiming, of sorts. A skinny, pubescent, young lady emerged from the cover of fat in one summer.

Parochial school does not necessarily set up an environment that encourages interest in sex. I managed to graduate from Saint Therese Academy with my virginity and heartstrings intact. High school was a different story, though.

In high school, I discovered how well drugs and alcohol help to anesthetize all kinds of maladies. When I was drunk, I felt powerful and angry. When I was on speed, I felt in control of my body and uninhibited about my sexuality. I could flirt with any girl I wanted to, as long as I had a boyfriend to fall back on. The drugs helped to take away the pain of being with men, an experience that left me feeling incompetent and unsatisfied. I had no clue that people had same-sex relationships without being struck by lightning or burning in hell, so I lost my virginity at the age of fourteen in a drunken stupor, convinced that it would make me feel in love with the boy and stop this insane fantasizing about women. What I felt was suicidal—my sister talked me off the balcony of our twenty-third-story vacation condo in Spain.

Always the A-student, I had no idea that my compulsive personality and numerous emotional troubles could send me on the downward spiral of addiction. But my love for crystal methamphetamine got me into a world of trouble. I was quietly asked not to return to my parochial high school, and I started attending Patrick Henry High School.

A striking brunette in my fourth period class caught my eye. With a French and Chinese background, Chrissy had a unique look that made me flush. She saw me walking home one day during the first week of school and offered me a ride. We lived only three blocks from each other, but had never before met. Our friendship was rapid and exciting. She was my first love.

Chrissy and I went to school together, wrote long letters to each other, talked on the phone, swam, rode her horse, partied and played together every day. It wasn't long before we shared our attraction for each other, and I stole my first kiss. It felt so good to be near her, I just didn't know how to be away from her.

Our awkward attempts at sexual encounters were both exhilarating and frustrating. We had no idea that other girls might be doing much the same thing. Our love for each other was so hidden and silenced that my older brother even tried to date Chrissy. He had no idea that she was *my* girlfriend.

It was painful to have such a secret. My use of crystal methamphetamine accelerated at a rapid pace and continued to deteriorate my mind, body, and spirit. I worked myself into an eight-hundred-dollar-a-day habit. I pushed away all ties with anyone who wasn't using drugs, and almost managed to estrange myself from Chrissy.

My parents took me to a family counselor who had to point out to them that I was on drugs. I was completely emaciated and deranged. It still stuns me that they didn't know I had such a big problem.

By some miracle, my parents decided to lock me up in Rancho Park Hospital in October 1987. I spent six months learning how to recognize, name, and take responsibility for my feelings and my boundaries. While this might come naturally to some, it was all brand new to me. I talked about my sexual abuse, my eating disorder, my disturbing upbringing, and started to come alive. I never talked about Chrissy, though. I didn't know how. I was sure they'd keep me locked up forever if they knew.

Chrissy visited me for three months, as often as regulation would allow. She brought me flowers, teddy bears, and pictures, and spent a lot of my passes with me. She wrote long and loving letters. I missed her desperately. But somehow, I was convinced that I had to pursue a relationship with a boy in order to complete my return to normalcy, so I broke her heart and she stopped coming to visit. The sweet trail of tender letters dried up. I lost her just like that and haven't seen her since.

I put all of my energy into staying clean and sober. I returned to Patrick Henry High and started a teen-support group. I dated a boy from Rancho Park for the next three years. He was a good friend and companion. We just had totally different sexual interests. I still wanted to be with a woman, but I didn't know how to do that. Eventually, my boyfriend and I broke up, and I stayed single for two years. I developed painful crushes on female teachers and straight girlfriends that left me feeling so pathetic and impotent. Then I met Laura. She was the manager of a popular coffeehouse I frequented with my friends. I knew that she was a lesbian, and I knew that she liked to flirt with me, but she was also gorgeous and intimidating. I had no idea how to approach her.

I happened to be at the coffeehouse the night someone brought her a balloon with "Happy Birthday" on it. Of course, I asked her about it. She told me that she was in an anonymous twelve-step program. I had no idea that we could have something in common, and I gained the confidence to talk openly with her. That led to flirting. After that, I came to the coffeehouse every day. We exchanged phone numbers. We made plans together. She invited me over. I went. She kissed me. I kissed her back.

Laura introduced me to San Diego's lesbigay [lesbian, bisexual, and gay] community, where there are dance clubs for same-sex couples. There is a gay Alano club in town where we can go to twelve-step meetings. There is an entire community of people here that loves us just the way we are. That feels right. That seems like the way it should be everywhere.

It bothers a lot of people that I call myself "bisexual." I have called myself bisexual since I was twelve. I don't claim that as a permanent label. I don't claim it is a transition phase. I don't know if I should suddenly be called a lesbian because I am so happy with Laura. I do not call myself bisexual because I need a man to satisfy me. I call myself bisexual because it's what I decided a long time ago, but I am also very much in love with a woman.

If there was one piece of advice I could give my fifteen-year-old self, it would be to call the nearest lesbian and gay community center. With support groups and community resources, they can point out all of the gay-friendly places in town, including under-twenty-one dance clubs. I can only imagine what a difference it would have made in my relationship with Chrissy if we had known of a public place where we could go dancing together. I can only imagine what a difference it would have made in my self-worth to walk into a community so full of love and acceptance.

ERIC, 21, Holbrook, New York

Hiding became my speciality. Involving myself in everything I could, attempting to fulfill the expectations of what family and friends thought would make me a "good" kid, putting on a smile whenever I was in public; it took several years before I could honestly smile. Right around that time I discovered the true meaning of honesty. More importantly, I discovered the true *value* of honesty.

I guess I've known I was gay all my life. The early years contained many of the classic experiences. In fifth grade, the guys and I would explore the idea of sex in the most childish ways. Sleepover parties were my favorite. Inevitably the conversation would turn to such topics as underwear or farting, but to fifth, sixth, and seventh graders, we might as well have been naked and breathing heavy. Occasionally, someone would be truly bold and moon the group. Oh, what fun!

Sleep-away camp lent itself to exploration as well. The summer between fourth and fifth grade I learned what an erection was. Six guys in a tent without a parental figure and instructed to go to bed had no intention of falling asleep until our eyelids felt like anvils. At some point, the conversation turned to sex. And that same friend who enjoyed mooning the guys also instructed us, using his own body for visual proof, as to what an erection was. Soon after, we were all erect, with very little inkling that what we were doing would be considered by some to be wrong. Of course, word soon leaked out of our activity, and only then did I learn that naked boys should not play together.

Boys and girls, though, were allowed to be naked together—when they grew up. YUCK! There was no way I would ever let that happen to me, but expectations said that someday I'd be a father. Easy solution—adoption! For years I told family and friends that I planned to adopt children, seeing as there were so many needy children out there.

Although I enjoyed playing baseball, joining Little League was also a means of hiding. In fact, I hid on the team for six years. Little boys are supposed to swing bats and get sweaty running around in the dirt, without getting nailed in the head with a hardball. Playing center field balanced out the activity that little boys should not be a part of, but which I loved: dancing! I took dance lessons for seven years. The classes were filled with girls, but I didn't care. Some of my best friends are girls.

Memories from high school consist of some fun times, but it seems now to have been a very shallow existence. I was not connected to anything, and yet I somehow managed to sweep up one scholarship award after another. This, of course, was a testament to my desire to do whatever possible to please those around me, and to balance out the eventual truth and horror of being gay.

One of the cruelest ways I hid from being found out was to join fellow classmates in the teasing of our twelfth-grade English teacher. None of us knew for sure that he was gay, but it did not stop us from being nasty in the comments we made behind his back. I regret having ever been a part of that. How unfortunate that society makes it so difficult for teachers to be healthy role models for students who could truly benefit from their experience. To my twelfth-grade English teacher: Please know that I am sorry, and that I'm trying.

Although it seemed as if the friends I had would be with me forever, this would not be the case. Ironically, many of the guys in my high-school group of friends have now come out of the closet as well, but at that time the last thing I would have ever dreamed about doing is uttering that I thought I might be gay.

College days arrived before I knew it, and I was still hiding. The four years had more ups and downs than the roughest of roller coasters. Hiding became an art. I involved myself with a plentitude of co-curricular activities, raising my hand to volunteer for everything as if my arm were filled with helium. Alcohol also seemed to work for a while, a short while. How fun to have an excuse for lowering my inhibitions! But I finally realized that crying after a few hours of laughing with friends did not balance out.

Surely God was the answer. I attended church regularly all my life, taught Sunday School, tried to sing in the choir, and was an officer of the youth group. At college I joined a group on campus that loved to praise Him and then discuss how horrible we all were for not being perfect. The rationale was that God loved us anyway. But the arrogant and destructive way in which the collective whole cast the word of God, as they saw it, down upon us would constantly push someone into feelings of inadequacy and self-loathing. It didn't seem healthy to hide among those believers, so I came back to secular living in search of a new hiding spot.

The best spot ever was behind my image as a "nice guy." For years people would tell me how they thought I'd make a great boyfriend. "No, I haven't had sex yet. I'm just waiting for the right girl. It's got to be special," I would say. I can't believe so many people bought it; or did they?

At a time when it seemed as if there was no place else to hide, life dealt me a hand that had to be played out, and it was time to bet it all. Friendships in college are intense. My friendships with two friends grew beyond just friends and on to love, and there was no place to hide.

The first relationship started while I was a freshman and Jonathan was a sophomore. We seemed to have so much in common. I wanted to spend every minute with him. The phone would ring, and my heart would skip beats. A knock at the door, and I'd get dizzy. A hug good-bye or for thanks, and I barely kept from passing out. We made each other laugh. We let each other cry. We fought intensely about nothing. I fell in love. Two years into it I let him know. He tried to be helpful, but he wanted to be just friends. I dug a hole and hid deeper than ever. It was unhealthy to be friends with him. I needed time apart from him, so I pissed him off. We barely spoke his last year at school.

Overlapping with this rocky affair was a relationship with the second love of my life. Rich and I were both juniors when my relationship with Jonathan crumbled, and when Rich told me he was gay.

My friend's coming out scared me so much that within a week I had a girlfriend, the only girlfriend I've ever had. We were together for just under two months. We fooled around, a little. Of course it felt good, but it felt empty. Hiding in a heterosexual relationship has to be the biggest lie I have ever told. One night at a party I realized it just wasn't going to work. The next morning my girlfriend and I decided to break it off. I talked to Rich about my feelings for him again and agreed to go to counseling. It was two weeks before semester break and I was grateful for the upcoming time away. The week before I left, I made one last attempt to clear things up with Jonathan.

Second semester junior year, life began again. Jonathan and Rich knew the truth. My counselor knew more than he probably wanted to. The next step was my ex-girlfriend. I couldn't have asked for a better response. Slowly, I added some more females to the list of the keepers of the secret. Every friendship grew stronger and stronger.

The summer before my senior year, I entered a new stage. One of the guys I worked with was openly gay. We worked for the college and both lived in the residence halls. Eventually, convenience brought us together. It took a month and a half of intense flirting and building passion. Our relationship was strictly physical and ended in in tense anger. Unfortunately, our lack of emotional attachment prevented either of us from protecting the other from the hurt. What did happen, however, was that I was brought into the realm of sexual activity, which inevitably changed my relationship with myself forever.

I'm at a point in my life where I can be honest with the people around me because I'm honest with myself. There is a great deal of value in honesty. The bonds that form between people who are able to speak the truth are stronger than steel. I can't imagine my life today if I were still in the closet. The air in there was getting too thin for the asthmatic that I am, anyway. However, I can remember back to the time when my place in the closet was the only safety I felt. I appreciate the path I traveled along before I turned the knob on the closet door. As I look into the hiding spots that kept me safe, I realize that safety and happiness are not equal.

My parents know I'm gay. We went through lots of tears and lots of questions. They are both concerned about my safety. They worry about AIDS and the close-minded people of this world. These fears are justifiable, and I know they're afraid because they genuinely love me. So I try to comfort them, but I also let them be concerned because that's what moms and dads are for and why we love them back.

My sister knows, and friends, co-workers, and acquaintances know, too. That's not everyone, but I don't know everything about everyone else either. All things take time.

God also knows that I'm gay, and I know in my heart that He loves me.

The best part of hide-and-go-seek is being found. That's when the excitement really builds, and for a while there is a lot of chasing around and avoiding being tagged or labeled "it." Eventually you reach base. Then you are safe *and* you are happy. Trust me. I've played the game. I've reached the base. Truth be told, I don't need to hide anymore.

2

on coming out

For the most part, lesbians and gays in the past went unnoticed by society. Of course, the "butch" lesbian or effeminate gay might have been labeled homosexual by the heterosexual population, but the vast majority simply blended in, not revealing publicly any details of their private lives. Effectively, they were "in the closet," jargon that is used to describe lesbians and gays who hide their sexual orientation. Privately, though, these closeted individuals often sought out hidden circles of homosexual life for socialization.[1] Their work lives were separate and distinct from their social lives, the two never mixing or overlapping out of a realistic fear of a loss of livelihood.

Even their social lives were segmented into "those-who-know" and "those-who-don't-know." As a teenager, I made a family visit to long-time friends, Warren and Norm. At one time, Warren had served with my father in the military, and he and my parents seemed to hit it off, at least on one level. When Warren moved in with Norm, invitations that would have been extended to Warren automatically included Norm. I recall, though, as we left their house on this particular occasion that my older brother, in his late twenties then, asked, "Do you think they're queers?" Both of my parents were aghast at the notion and explained, "Their relationship is strictly financial. They can't possibly be queers; they're both nice people." Obviously, my parents were in the "those-who-don't-know" group, because years later they discovered the true nature of Warren's and Norm's relationship. Indeed, an entire underground network of homosexual acquaintances, whose private lives my parents were unaware of, unfolded. While the gay individuals were privy to each other's homosexuality, their secret had been kept from my parents—and for a just reason. Upon discovery, my parents excluded them from their circle of friends, in spite of "friendships" that had endured twenty years and longer. The "nice people" suddenly had become tainted.

Generations of lesbians and gays knew that rejection was the probable reaction that heterosexuals would have, should private lives become public. "The closet" became a safe place to store the gay aspect of one's identity. But harboring secrets is injurious to one's emotional well-being and allows false stereotypes to persist. Members of the younger generation have realized that beliefs many heterosexuals hold of lesbians and gays don't describe them. The stereotypes are exaggerated or simply false. Hoping to enlighten the ignorant and misinformed, they began to "come out of the closet" by speaking openly of their sexuality. Today, at gay pride parades and celebrations, a chant may be heard from coast to coast: "We're here, we're queer—and you better get used to it."

Such self-acceptance doesn't occur overnight. For most, the journey toward acknowledging that they are both lesbian or gay and good human beings is a long one. At the first inkling that they may have same-sex attractions, most lesbians and gays deny it. They deny it not only to others, but also to themselves. They are aware of the negative images associated with homosexuality, and they can't believe themselves to be so vile.

But attractions are attractions. When the reality of their same-sex desires begins to set in, the next impulse is to *repair* the problem. Some seek repair in the form of psychiatric counseling. Others turn to their religion.

When repair doesn't work—there's no solid evidence that it does—then individuals may *avoid* the issue altogether. Some become promiscuous with the opposite sex, rationalizing that if they engage in heterosexual sex then their homosexual feelings will go away. They may bury themselves in school work or hobbies as a means of avoiding encounters with the opposite sex. They may even take a visible stance against homosexuality, engaging in anti-gay slurs or physical attacks. Many attempt to escape through alcohol and drug abuse.

Most find that they can't avoid their same-sex attractions indefinitely. What follows is a period of *redefinition*. That is, they may define their attraction to an individual of the same gender as an isolated experience, or they may take on the label of *bisexual*. While it is true that many individuals find themselves attracted equally to both men and women and are genuinely bisexual in orientation, some who are gay or lesbian in orientation find the *bisexual* label less intimidating than an admission of exclusivity. For these gays and lesbians, identifying themselves as bisexual is a "safety net," a way of allowing for some same-sex attraction while conforming at the same time to society's expectations that they be heterosexual. Discussing bisexuality in *Children of Horizons*, Gilbert Herdt and Andrew Boxer wrote, "[F]or many youth, though by no means all, bisexuality is a social phase, a certain developmental step, into coming out."[2] Similarly, some claim "It's only a phase," while others suffer from what one San Diego State University freshman called the "Boy-was-I-drunk-last-night syndrome." Redefinition attempts to keep the label of homosexuality at distance.

Eventually, though, feelings—whether bisexual or homosexual—are likely to catch up with an individual, and he or she will *accept* them for what they are.[3] For some, the process may be relatively speedy; for others, it may take years. Aaron Fricke and Mel White might represent opposite ends of the spectrum. Aaron was sixteen when he came to terms with his homosexuality; in a celebrated case, he later successfully brought suit against his Rhode Island high school for the right to bring a male escort to his senior prom.[4] Mel, on the other hand, managed to bury his sexuality until he was forty.[5] The father of two children, he was married prior to accepting his sexual orientation and worked in the inner circles of the vehemently antigay evangelists Jerry Falwell and Pat Robertson, and also for Billy Graham.

It has been said that lesbian and gay youths "come out in a society that places them at risk of many forms of bigotry, and they know it."[6] Given this, you might think that they would prefer to stay in the closet. Certainly, a number of heterosexuals would prefer it that way. A common response from the straight population is, "Why do they have to make so much noise about it? I'm sick of having homosexuality shoved in my face."

Imagine for an instant, though, that the world were predominantly homosexual. Films, books, and plays only depict homosexuals. Advertising is directed at homosexual singles or couples. It is commonplace to see homosexual couples holding hands and acknowledging affection for each other, but heterosexual displays of caring are ridiculed, or worse, cause for imprisonment. Couples with children are denied parenthood purely because of their heterosexuality. Businesses fire heterosexual employees, not because of incompetence, but for their sexual orientation. Heterosexuals are denied military service to their country, again not because of incompetence, but because it is "bad for morale." Imagine that the majority society—homosexuals—refuses to acknowledge that heterosexuality exists; and when it does, it paints an abnormal picture of it. How might the heterosexual population react under such circumstances?

Lesbians and gays grow up and live in a society balanced toward heterosexuality. It is only natural that they are vocal about misconceptions, half-truths, and fair and equal treatment. Herdt and Boxer explain it this way: "Youth who are coming out today keep harping on their newfound identities because, if they do not, common assumptions of heterosexuality return to gain sway: 'We are not who you think we are; in fact, we are gay and lesbian and proud of it,' they retort."[7] And so

COMING OUT

It is difficult to know the best approach, if there is one, for revealing same-sex desires to parents, and parents don't know what to do once they've been informed. Many parents feel inadequate. Most lack accurate knowledge about homosexuality. P-FLAG—Parents, Families and Friends of Lesbians and Gays—is an organization with chapters worldwide that strives to support sexual-minority youths and their parents with factual, accurate information. Before you "come out" to your parents, consider contacting P-FLAG. Information it can provide may be a good first step toward gaining their understanding.

P-FLAG
Suite 1030
1101-14th Street, NW
Washington, DC 20005
202/638-4200
pflagntl@aol.com

they come out, and will keep on coming out, until the myths and misconceptions held by the dominant group are put to rest.

Coming out is one of the bravest acts that sexual-minority teenagers can make. They must weigh the potential damage of remaining closeted against the risks of coming out. If they decide to come out, friends are usually the first to be told and parents are often the last. Beyond rejection, youths say that "they have to fear harassment and violence. . . . Parents sometimes react with anger to the knowledge of their children's sexual desires."[8] So harsh is the reaction of some parents that teenagers call it "extreme hostility," and many have found themselves facing "sudden homelessness" upon revealing their sexual identities.[9] In addition to the reaction of friends and family, some youths face ostracism by entire communities: "One study of multicultural gay and lesbian youth in Toronto found that when minority youths had come out to parents, the youths' relationships to their entire ethnic communities changed."[10] Yet in spite of these risks, most youths "feel that coming out has had a positive impact on their self-esteem."[11]

Coming out would be easier for teenagers if there were a strong base of support. Usually, though, such a support system is lacking.[12] Even adult homosexuals turn a blind eye toward the challenges that young lesbians and gays face. In part, this is because religious conservatives cry "recruitment" or "seduction" when they try to intervene, but also many have simply forgotten what it was like to be young and gay and isolated in what fifteen-year-old Christopher Rempel describes as "redneck farmer hell."[13]

Regardless of whether they live in the outback or an urban center, the closet is isolating for most lesbian and gay youths. Though full of risks, coming out seems to awaken a more positive sense of self-esteem.

SHULA, 17, Northfield, Massachusetts

Everyone was sleeping except me. I had gone to bed at eleven, the freshmen bedtime, but after listening to my roommate mumble in peaceful sleep for an hour, I had decided that I had to resolve the questions tugging at me. Quietly getting out of bed, I went to sit on the tile floor of the bathroom with pencil and paper, forcing myself to write down the words, "I think I'm gay." No one else was awake; I felt safe enough to admit my fears to myself. Once I had dealt with the fact that I was attracted to women, I saw my next step as a choice: Would I try to ignore it as I had for years, hoping it would just go away, or would I be strong enough to overcome the homophobia around me and simply let myself be what I instinctively knew I was? When I finally went to bed at 3:00 A.M., I decided to write an anonymous letter to the only gay student I knew of at my school because I'd done all the thinking one person could do. Even though I was in the unusual position of having a gay mother, I was still so much affected by the antigay messages in the media, in the government, and from my peers, that I was terrified of being a lesbian.

A gay teacher I met once said, "I don't choose whether I'm gay. I can choose whether or not I'm going to be miserable about it." Since the time I wrote this letter, I have come out first to my friends, one by one, and then to my whole school. Three years ago, I desperately wished to be straight; now, I love the unique outlook on life I have as a seventeen-year-old lesbian. I've met many wonderful, supportive gay people. The first of these was the sophomore whose response to my letter arrived in my mailbox precisely on my fifteenth birthday.

[What follows is the letter a 14-year-old Shula wrote to Stephen, and the response it drew.]

Dear Stephen,
I have a very strange favor to ask of you. No, you don't know who I am. I'm a student here and I think I'm gay. Basically, I'm really in need of correspondence with someone but there isn't anyone I can talk to; you are the only person on this campus who I'm absolutely positive is gay. Also, while my mother is a lesbian, I can't really talk to her because we don't tend to tell each other things. And there's one more problem that keeps me reluctant to just come out and tell her (or anyone else): I'm not, at this point, completely positive.

That is why I decided on you. If at all possible, could you write back to Box K72 (or find another student willing to do so)?

About a year ago (just before my fourteenth birthday), I started speculating about whether I was gay. It wasn't something I had foreseen for me; I'd always expected to marry a wonderful man and live in a nice house with our beautiful children, etc., etc. There followed a year of recurring worries which I tried to fight off. Frankly (no offense), the gay community is not one of which I am always terribly eager to be a part. And yet at the same time, I can see myself being happy in it. Trying to sort out my sexual feelings, I would try to catch my brain unawares: Okay, brain, think of sex. What comes to mind, a man or a woman? And I got a good deal of both. I fluctuated all the time; I had had my middle school crushes on male classmates, like anyone else, except that the guys I had chosen were no one's, including my own, idea of good-looking or ideal in any way.

When I was very, very little (five, maybe six), I had a couple of dreams that scared me; they weren't exactly sexual, but they were certainly dealing with women in maybe a "presexual" way. The particulars aren't really worth explaining, but when I remembered the dreams, I knew somehow that I couldn't tell anyone about them, that it was an indication that there was something "different" and "wrong" about me. It was before my mother's "partner" moved in and before I knew what "gay" meant or that any such thing existed.

But I can argue with myself the other way convincingly too. Look in my middle-school journals and you see the typical adolescent attractions. Believe me. And just this year, for fun, I learned how to say "I want a man" in ten languages—because I did, and I still do, at least a part of me. How is this possible?

After a year of fighting myself, I decided last Tuesday to simply give in and face it. After all, the fact that I had to fight it at all for so long seemed an indication that there was no point in doing so. I felt a hell of a lot better after reaching this point, but now I'm still questioning it. How can I possibly know when I'm only this young? How can I know enough to be able to reach a decision that will change my life so drastically? But it's impossible to ignore. And if I can make this choice, where do I go now? How do I proceed with life from that point onward?

I'm leaving this school next year for a number of good reasons, but one that entered slightly into my decision that nobody knows is that I want to be somewhere where I'm less afraid of this dilemma. Good lord, my friends here are all homophobic Christians with model families; they are very nice people but not of terribly wide horizons. (I keep wondering, how would people, not only these but everyone I know, respond.) Perhaps you have noticed that this campus in general is not a particularly liberal one.

What I need, I think, is to hear from someone else—how their brain worked, how they decided, how they knew, what made them think they were gay in the first place. I'll be so grateful if you can write back or find another student who will. It's so difficult when all I can do is think in circles for hours. Every day I look in the mirror and I wonder if gay people can tell I'm a lesbian even if I'm not sure of it myself. In the past, I've prided myself (no pun intended) on my ability to recognize gay people. The only person I'm unsure of now is myself.

I REALLY appreciate your help.

— Box K72

Dear Box K72,
You do not know who I am, but Stephen is a good
friend of mine and he shared your letter with me.
Even though I believe he plans on writing back, I
felt suddenly that I must. Just about two months
ago I began coming to terms with my own homosexuality. It was scary, but having Stephen to
come out to first was helpful. I admitted to him
that I had an attraction toward men, but did not
make any concrete judgments on myself.

I, too, had crushes throughout middle school
on girls who weren't terribly attractive, and I could
never understand why the other guys got so
turned on by these gorgeous, blond-bombshell
types. They did nothing for me personally. I had a
fairly sexual relationship with a girl just this past
summer, which was pleasant and comforting, but
not fulfilling. I always had a difficult time keeping
my eyes off attractive, bare-chested men.

Life in the gay community does not strike me
as a very good option because of the narrow-
minded society around it. I still wish I could share
my life with a woman—to please my parents and
a part of myself which wants to please that nar-
row-minded society.

I still retain an emotional attraction to women.
A lot of this has to do with the fact that I can relate better to straight women than I can to straight
men. I have some wonderful women in my life,
and I find myself wanting to get intimate with
them. I have no male lover and though I continue
to long for these straight men, hoping they're really bisexual or gay and just haven't dealt with it
yet, I find myself wanting a woman as well.

Anyway, I take life day by day. I've had my fears and my share of denial about my sexuality for a long time. Now, I just lust after that which gives me the most pleasure. I don't over lust after women, which leads me to believe that I'm not bisexual.

I still have not told my parents, and I'm afraid of their reaction. I'm rather jealous that you have a gay parent because at least you'll have guaranteed support from one corner. I expect my mom to react the same way she did when I said "I think I might be gay" when I was in sixth grade. She and my dad in unison laughed and said, "No, you're not!" I hope they're good about it.

I still have a hard time labeling myself as "gay," and I still feel more at ease in the arms of a woman. (I've had one homosexual experience.) I can only do what feels right. If at some point sleeping with a woman feels right, then I'll probably do it, but somehow I don't think it will be as satisfying.

I'm not really out on campus. I'm only out to a few people who I care about, to whom I want to be able to talk openly. Homosexual people who have been completely out and obvious on this campus don't have very positive experiences, which leads me to believe that I don't want to be out to the campus. There may come a point when a lot of people know, but I don't think I want it that way. I don't want my experience here to be a miserable one.

I know that I'm gay. You can know by which kind of body you get aroused by, I suppose. It all comes down to a real innate attraction. It isn't a conscious choice, but rather a subconscious orientation. Straight people have an innate orientation for the opposite sex. It doesn't mean that they are incapable of having a homosexual relationship. My being gay doesn't make me incapable of having a heterosexual relationship.

I have fun with your "gaydar" [gay radar], but don't confuse it, as I have, with wishful thinking. Go with what feels right; that's the best advice anyone can tell you. Feelings will always win out over words and rationalizations. Rationalizing and looking for reasons why you're not gay aren't going to help. The sooner you allow yourself to lust after beautiful women you see pass by or on TV, the sooner you'll be able to be content with yourself again. And don't even try to understand the world around you until you understand yourself. You're not "a lesbian." You're just a person like the rest of us. Society gives the label. Your sexuality is a big part of your life, but don't forget it's not the only part. Just think of it as something that makes you all the more unique.

—a friend

TREY, 19, Chapel Hill, North Carolina

The following essay was written when Trey was 16, to celebrate his first year out.

CONTEMPLATIONS OF THE FIRST YEAR OUT[14]
Yesterday I was going through my closet, chucking clothes that no longer fit, trying on things that once had been too big, attempting to squeeze into clothes clearly marked "Large" before realizing they were so old that the "Large" was a child's size, when my Scout uniform fell on the floor at my feet.

I picked it up and held it in my hands for the first time in—how long?—a year. Yes, it's been a year now. I looked at the familiar patches and in-

signia; the council shoulder patch I had had since my very first Cub uniform. The tattered "2" in white stitching on a red background that had been the only troop number to stay with me all those eight years. The Order of the Arrow pocket flap, designating I was a member of the Brotherhood of Honor Campers. The blue and gold shoulder strap for all to see that I had led my own den of Cub Scouts.

Over the right chest was the light blue space-shuttle emblem that showed I had attended the National Scout Jamboree. I fondly remembered, as I looked at that patch, the eight days of living with seventy-nine thousand other Scouts from around the world, of marching *en masse* to the great amphitheater to hear the president speak, of doing everything from volleyball to drafting to running a BMX course.

And there, on the left pocket, was my shining achievement, the emblem symbolizing the hard work of people as diverse as Ross Perot and Steven Spielberg—the oval patch, red, white, and blue, with the border of silver thread. It read in proud, silver lettering: Eagle Scout. Boy Scouts of America. Above it dangled the silver eagle, attached to the shirt with a red, white, and blue ribbon sporting three palms showing that I had not been content to win my Eagle and leave.

It's been just over a year since my last Scout meeting.

So much has happened in the year since that day when I looked at myself in the mirror and said, "Face it. You're gay." In that year my friends have become enemies; my rivals, friends. My political beliefs have been turned upside down. My entire values system, the way I decide who is a person I would like to know better and who I would rather not, has changed radically. In this year, I've come out to, at last count, thirty-seven people I know, and hundreds, perhaps thousands I don't know through a computer network. I have started a gay youth group and watched it flounder through lack of interest. I have told a table of complete strangers during the course of a political discussion that I am gay. I have experienced an online [computer] romance. I've worn a pink triangle in a fundamentalist Southern Baptist church. I've worn a pink triangle at Walt Disney World. I have watched my parents cry and heard them ask, "How did I fail you?" I have been put into psychotherapy in an attempt to "cure" me of my homosexuality. I've stayed up late at night listening to my father sob and tried to ignore his not eating for a week. I've been harassed by teachers and cruel students, and been "outed" by a faculty member at my high school.

This year, I have made better friends than I knew were possible, friends who care about who I am, not what I am. I spent hour upon hour talking to one of my teachers, who began to attend P-FLAG [Parents, Families and Friends of Lesbians and Gays] meetings as my friend. (Two months later he attended as a P rather than an F, his son having come out to him.) I learned that it is indeed possible to express attraction for a friend of the same sex and not have him go running.

And in the past year, life went on. I did other things. I was an extra in a movie. I graduated from high school. I was accepted to college. I won fifty dollars in an essay contest. I burned all my flyers left from my work in the Jesse Helms campaign. I read all the Armistead Maupin novels at the library. I taught the advanced calculus classes at my school. I published the school newspaper and the underground paper at the same time.

It has been the best year of my life. My self-esteem and my happiness have increased a hundredfold. I have a set of friends who care about me. I can look at gorgeous guys who walk past me shirtless on this hot summer day without pangs of guilt.

Do I have regrets? Of course. I wish I had hidden the book *Growing Up Gay in the South* better the day my parents searched my room. I wish I had thought to come out to my teacher's son. I wish I had asked my former best friend what he thought about my gayness instead of avoiding him for months after I came out. I wish this could have been my fifth anniversary rather than my first.

With a sigh, I started to put back the old familiar green-and-khaki uniform where it has always been, on the hanger in the very back of my closet. There were dark spots on the uniform shirt, making the khaki a muddy dark brown. Mildew? No, it was wet. Tears were streaming down my face.

It's a bit hard to say good-bye to what has been, even when what is to be is far better. A year ago, I was comfortable. I did not have to worry about my parents calling me for another shouting match about my sexuality. I didn't have to contend with explaining the birds and the bees to another relative every time I turned around. A year ago, life was easier.

But today, I like who I am.

CHRISTOPHER, 19, Greenwich, Connecticut

I think the one thing that is really striking about the queer community, as I call all of us whether we be closeted or out, conservative or liberal, apolitical or radical, is that it is extraordinarily diverse. Queer people come from all walks of life, are of all races, and have all different kinds of experiences. Who am I to be saying this?

My name is Christopher, and I'm currently nineteen. It wasn't easy getting to where I am now. I'm from Greenwich, Connecticut, a predominantly white, upper-middle to upper-class, conservative town that isn't very tolerant of anyone who is different from the perceived "norm." My family consisted of mother, father, and brother. I was the second child. While very loving, my family was also homophobic. My brother and father were constantly telling jokes about "fudge-packers" and "faggots." Thus, throughout my childhood, I was bombarded with homophobic remarks, not only from society around me, but also from those closest to me.

Around seventh grade, I first felt the stirrings of my sexuality, and it turned out that sexuality meant that I would be attracted solely to people of my own sex. It took me a good four years of agonizing and dealing with my own internalized homophobia before I was ready to tell anyone else. Those years were hellish, and I became paranoid about anyone finding out. I was so worried that I didn't develop any significant friendships and began to withdraw emotionally from my family, not telling them any of the things I was feeling for fear of what they would do to me if they knew.

By the time I was in tenth grade, I had no friends who were close to me at all. Then I met someone whom I trusted for one reason or another. She seemed like a really nice, understanding, liberal person. Her name was Kendra. We became friends, and after several months of knowing her, I felt comfortable enough to tell her. We were talking on the phone, and I directed her Into a question-and-answer game where she asked me if I was gay. I answered truthfully, but I didn't say, "I am gay." I couldn't tell her that, because I couldn't make those words form on my lips. It is really amazing to think that our society is so homophobic that it can take someone who is gay years before being able to say the words out loud. Kendra was taken aback. She said that she had to go and that she would call me back. I thought that I had upset her and that we would no longer be friends, but it turned out that she just needed some time to think. She had been interested in me as more than just a friend, and I had just destroyed that possibility for her. My paranoia and assumption that no one would ever accept me turned out to be wrong in Kendra's case, but I still felt it was a good assumption to keep, just to be safe. Kendra called me back two days later and apologized. She was my support structure for the remainder of high school. If I hadn't had her support, I don't know what I would have done.

In December of my senior year in high school, I told my mother, after having what amounted to a nervous breakdown one day. On that day, the utter hopelessness of my situation, as I saw it, hit me. I thought that I was never going to meet anyone like me, because I would never be able to tell my parents or deal with my situation. I thought that my parents would disown me, and that I would never be able to live a normal life. All of these thoughts had been ruminating in my mind for a long time, and they exploded forth that afternoon. I had sat down at the piano to play, and I burst into tears spontaneously. I couldn't stop crying. My mother was the only other person at home at the time, and she asked me what was wrong. I decided at that moment that I couldn't go on without telling her, regardless of the consequences. My recklessness, as my paranoid nature made it out to be, turned out to be the best thing for me. I was lucky. My mother accepted me for who I was, and agreed to help me deal with it. She promised not to tell my brother or father until I was ready to tell them myself. So, with my mother and Kendra being the only two people who knew that I was gay, and never having met another gay, lesbian, or bisexual person, I went to MIT [Massachusetts Institute of Technology] in the fall of 1992 as a freshman.

During Residence and Orientation Week at MIT, freshmen choose where they want to live. They have the option of either living in a dorm or joining an ILG (Independent Living Group), most of which are fraternities and all of which have houses of their own, either on or off campus. I met a lot of people I really liked at one fraternity, Theta Chi, and pledged that week. It turned out that they were as homophobic as my father and brother. One of them, in fact, said at one point that "people who are that way should be taken out and shot." Given my paranoia and my fear of being found out, this was not what I wanted to hear. I was afraid that if I told them, they would beat me up, or worse, tell my father, because I thought he would withdraw his support if he knew. So, I didn't leave Theta Chi. I stayed for the first semester and felt guilty that I wasn't strong enough to stand up to them. I often defended gays when someone said something derogatory, though I didn't do it as a gay man. I defended gays as a supposedly "open-minded" straight person.

I had a rough first term at MIT. My father wrote me a letter saying that he and my mother loved me and understood that college was difficult and that I should hang in there. I wrote him back, telling him that college wasn't the thing that was giving me difficulty. Impulsively, I decided that I wanted to get it over with. I told him that we would discuss what was giving me difficulty and causing me to distance myself from him when I got home for winter break. Well, apparently, the tone of my letter was serious enough that my father didn't want to wait. He asked my mother if she knew what was bothering me; and because he wouldn't take no for an answer, she told him my secret. Then she called me and said that they were coming up to Boston to talk with me about it. I flipped out. I thought I had destroyed everything.

My parents showed up the next day. They picked me up at Theta Chi, and we drove to a hotel to talk. My father, who I had assumed was going to disown me right then and there, began by quoting the Bible. He quoted a passage which said that love conquers all things. He said that he accepted me for who I was, and that I had changed nothing. It would be difficult for him, but he was willing to support me.

Even though my parents turned out to be supportive, it would take me over a year and a half to start reestablishing the emotional bonds I had broken with them. I desperately wanted parents when my parents didn't know, but I had emotionally divorced myself from them. I stopped caring about them a whole lot because I hated them for the things they said, or didn't say. I hated my brother and father for saying cruel things, and I hated my mother for not defending gays and lesbians against the things that were said. After my parents knew, the bitterness and hatred I had directed at them began to subside, and the love that was always there began to show through.

Even though my parents were supportive, I still had internalized homophobia because society teaches gay people to hate themselves. I decided that I didn't want to risk telling the people at Theta Chi, because I was still very much paranoid. I thought that they would bash me if I told them. But after the fall term, I moved into a dorm. It was difficult to walk out on friends I had made and who seemed sincerely interested in being closer to me, but I thought that they wouldn't want to know me or would be disgusted by me if they knew. So, I left.

I lived in a dorm over IAP (Independent Activities Period, a month between the semesters at MIT where you can do whatever you want). During that time, I went to a film series called "Homophobia and Billy's Life to Live." They showed an edited version of the episodes from "One Life to Live" which dealt with homophobia that year. The film series was cathartic and made me think. I decided that I wanted to take the next step and come out at MIT.

The first thing I did was to go to a GaMIT-sponsored dance (Gays, Lesbians, Bisexuals, and Transgenders at MIT). It was strange. Men were dancing with men and women were dancing with women. I sat there for twenty minutes just staring in awe. I was finally in an environment where I could be who I was and not be an object of curiosity or derision. It was a liberating experience— and a shock to my system. I met someone there who I had seen at the film series, and he invited me to a GaMIT study break. I went.

It was at that study break that I met my first boyfriend, Tom. He was a member of another fraternity, Tau Epsilon Phi (TEP), but he was open about it there, and no one minded. He invited me to a midnight social event called "Hot Cocoa," which was to be held the next evening.

At Hot Cocoa, GaMIT people left the ground floor of the house with Tom and went to his room on the third floor. It was a room with four beds situated above four desks. Suspended from the beds and attached to the opposite wall was a huge fish net. Up to twenty-two people could sit comfortably in the net and be suspended six feet in the air.

There we were, hanging six feet above the floor in the net, talking. I thought Tom was very cute, so I decided to take a risk. I lay down next to him in the net, and after several hours of talking with everyone, I rested my head on his shoulder. He didn't pull away. We lay there for a while. Later, after everyone had left the room, we went downstairs to the front room and continued talking. We talked until 5:00 A.M. about our lives, how difficult it was to be closeted, and what we wanted from our futures. Tom and I clicked. I felt extremely comfortable around him, and felt as if I could tell him anything. At one point during our conversation, he put his hand on my knee to comfort me, or so he told me later. Well, never having been close to anyone whom I felt this way toward or with whom I could express my feelings, I was excited. I leaned over, and we kissed. We consummated our budding relationship that night, joyfully. Having repressed my sexuality for so long, it was an amazing experience to physically express it. It confirmed what I already knew: that I really WAS gay, that it felt comfortable to be gay, and that I could express myself sexually as a gay man. It was a relief, and a giant step toward accepting who I am.

From that day forward, Tom and I were inseparable. We entered into what was essentially a marriagelike relationship that was very serious and involved. We talked about everything with each other, supported each other, and had fun together. I lived in my dorm for that semester in word only. In truth, I spent every night at TEP with Tom. We grew very close over the seven months that we were together, but in the end it turned out that, even though we loved each other, we were different kinds of people. He wanted more independence than I did, and I wanted to explore other possibilities before settling down into something so devoted. So, we broke up. It was difficult, but we both survived it and are still friends. I pledged

TEP the following year, and currently live here as a fraternity brother.

In the months after Tom and I broke up, I had a series of flings and abortive attempts at relationships. I found out to my chagrin that what Tom and I had was special. It isn't easy to find someone who is different enough to be fascinating, but similar enough to be compatible, and attractive enough to provoke interest in more than just close friendship. What I experienced with Tom, I would legitimately call love. I cared for him deeply and still do. When I was going out with him, I cared enough about him to give my life for him. Feelings like these are universal, and it shouldn't matter if you're gay or straight. I hope to discover them again one day when I find someone who fascinates me as much as he did.

3
on high school

High school marks a rite of passage for adolescents. It's a time of football rallies, harvest balls, and first cars. Bonds that will last lifetimes are forged here, as are decisions that will impact on futures. High schools have an essential role in American society. But they also play a central role in the perpetuation of *homophobia*, or anti-gay sentiment, and it is "condoned or at least tolerated by many school authorities."[1] Although dedicated to educating and enlightening, high schools generally have passed on old myths about homosexuality and shirked their responsibility to serve the needs of those entrusted to their care. To be a high-school student, and lesbian or gay, is to be ignored, denied, and, at times, even abused.[2]

Researchers Hetrick and Martin wrote, "At a time when heterosexual adolescents are learning how to socialize, young gay people are learning how to hide."[3] No one teaches lesbian and gay youths how to navigate the surrounding heterosexual world, let alone the homosexual one, so it should come as no surprise that they often withdraw from school activities and—far too frequently—from life itself. If they don't withdraw, they develop a strategy of deception that touches every relationship they have, including family.

Why are so few lesbian and gay students open about their sexual identities in high school? In a word, the answer is *survival*. According to a recent U.S. Department of Justice report, lesbians and gays are the most frequent victims of hate violence, and school is its primary setting.[4] Lesbian and gay teenagers, and those perceived to be lesbian or gay, are subjected to a wide range of abuses, from verbal to physical, and it emanates not only from other students, but also from teachers and school administrators. One researcher charges, "High schools may be the most homophobic institutions in American society, and woe be to anyone who would challenge the heterosexist premises on which they operate."[5] Although this charge may be slightly overstated—it fails to take into account the considerable hate emanating from conservative fundamental religious groups and their leaders—lesbian and gay teenagers face a tremendous challenge in the typical high-school arena.

At the very least, silence by teachers and administrators is one of those challenges, and it is the one most easily addressed. A student who hurls the epithet *nigger* or *spic* at another student is typically punished. What happens to the youngster who calls another youth *queer*, *faggot*, *joto*, *dyke*, or *lesbo*? Sadly, most school officials take a position of silence, and thereby, give unspoken approval of such behavior. In a survey at one Massachusetts high school, more than 97 percent of the students said they had heard anti-gay comments within their school.[6] Most of these comments, if not all, went unchallenged, unprotested. We have seen the result of silence in Nazi Germany, and it explains a slogan popular in the lesbian and gay community: Silence = Death.

Unfortunately, there is another kind of silence. There is an overwhelming lack of mention in textbooks and school curricula of contributions made by lesbians and gays. Lesbian and gay youngsters go through school with no lesbian or gay heroes to look up to or emulate. Reference to homosexuality is scant, if at all, and then only in brief passages in biology or sex-education classes. It's not surprising that many of these young people view themselves as anomalies, the only one of their kind, and seek refuge in books or drugs and alcohol. Even when lesbian and gay youths have knowledge of gay gathering places such as in San Francisco, Chicago, and New York, inability to access others of their kind, even if through the context of books, leads to a sense of isolation and a feeling of inadequacy. Some researchers call the absence of minority representation in literature and television "symbolic annihilation" by the dominant group.[7] It is an attempt to keep minorities "in their place," if you will, and was experienced by African-Americans, who were oddly unrepresented in history and literature prior to the civil rights movement. It has been experienced by Hispanic Americans. And it can be seen in attempts to keep homosexuality invisible by some members of conservative religious groups.

We must protect our children and youth from this homosexual recruitment. . . . You don't want to tolerate sin. You don't want to tolerate perversion. . . . We stand upon the principles of Judeo-Christian values and beliefs. And there is no way we are going to say that homosexuality is viable.

—Rev. Lou Sheldon
Traditional Values Coalition

Ballyhooing *recruitment* as the rallying cry, some well-financed conservative groups—such as the American Family Association, the Traditional Values Coalition, and Focus on the Family—disseminate false "statistics" and misleading "expert opinions" to paint a highly inflammatory and negative image of homosexuals.[8] Then in well-organized efforts to excise, or *symbolically annihilate*, homosexuality, they challenge any curriculum that fosters respect for the enormous contributions made by lesbians and gays. In so doing, they undermine the self-esteem, the self-worth, and the self-confidence of lesbian and gay adolescents.

Even the most well-intentioned or innocent mention of homosexuality is subject to the censor's ax. In an age when Acquired Immune Deficiency Syndrome (AIDS) has reached epidemic proportions, threatening both homosexuals and heterosexuals, at least one California school system has fallen sway to pressure from conservative religious forces to remove references about homosexuality and "safe-sex" practices from its sex education program. In another symbolic annihilation, the much acclaimed and award-winning book *Lives of the Musicians* was restricted to grade 7 and up in large part because it mentioned that Tchaikovsky was homosexual. The book's author was brave enough to question the decision of the book selection committee; and the committee, upon second review, back-pedaled to restrict the book to grades 5 and up. Lesbians and gays report that "difference" was sensed at a very early age. Knowledge of the contributions that lesbians and gays have made to society can make a positive impact on young people who are feeling different from their peers and unable to qualify that difference. Moreover, it can help end the damaging stereotypes held by heterosexual students. Restricting access to this knowledge is a form of censorship and dereliction of educational responsibility.

The conspiracy of silence surrounding homosexuality leaves lesbian and gay youths abandoned in their school environments because it negates their sexual identities.[9] They are denied the history and literature that reflects themselves, and they are not provided any positive lesbian and gay role models in person. So distorted is homosexuality and so anti-gay is the environment, that lesbian and gay teachers usually opt to dwell in their closets. Armistead Maupin, author of the popular novels in the *Tales of the City* series, takes a dim view of their reticence. He asks, "Have you forgotten already how much it hurt to be 14 and gay and scared to death of it?"[10] Yet, one can understand why many lesbian and gay teachers choose the safety of the closet. In Martinez, California, Morello Park Elementary School had to seek a court order in 1994 to keep Valerie Russo from disrupting classes.[11] A parent, Russo merely *suspected* that a teacher might be gay and made such an habitual nuisance of herself that teaching became impossible. The misconceptions and "halo of hate," as one writer calls it, that surround the topic of homosexuality make it difficult for lesbian and gay teachers to be positive role models at any level of education when those who are merely suspected are subject to harassment and, even worse, termination of employment.[12]

Schools will have to change if they are to become equally supportive and accessible to gay and lesbian youths. One researcher calls for them "to focus further

Censorship, like charity, should begin at home; but unlike charity, it should end there.

—Clare Booth Luce

on the needs of young people, rather than be exclusively concerned with community response."[13] This may offend individual parents who may not want to admit that their children are sexual, or *homosexual*. It may draw the ire of conservative religious groups, who may label a book or curriculum "inappropriate for the community." These same conservative groups may push to withhold public funds from school systems that have policies of inclusion. But public schools encompass an enormous diversity, and should embrace all aspects of it. To do less is to shirk their responsibility. In most communities, not everyone is white or African-American, not everyone is Christian, and not everyone is heterosexual.

It is true that public schools are dealing with reduced revenues and an increased presence of conservative "watchdog" groups and would-be censors, but their principal duty is to serve children—and not just heterosexual children. Lesbian and gay youths are arguably the most at-risk and "most underserved students in the entire educational system."[14]

Yet, not all is bleak. In the past several years, some responsible school systems have realized that their lesbian and gay students have not been served. Curriculum has been implemented, and not without some

GAY AND LESBIAN STUDENT RIGHTS BILL—
MASSACHUSETTS, 1993

No person shall be excluded from or discriminated against in admission to a public school of any town, or in obtaining the advantages, privileges and courses of study of such public school on account of race, color, sex, religion, national origin, or sexual orientation.

controversy, that at least attempts to comfort lesbian and gay students and children of lesbian and gay adults. Dr. Virginia Uribe founded Project 10, an intervention program for lesbian and gay youths, in Los Angeles Unified School District. Also in Los Angeles, the EAGLES Center exists as a school for lesbians and gays who find the traditional high school too uncomfortable. Its counterpart in New York is the Harvey Milk School. Some school systems are even sponsoring alternative proms for graduating lesbian and gay students and their friends.[15] And most notably, Massachusetts became the first state in the nation to pass a Gay and Lesbian Student Rights Bill, in December 1993.[16] Admirably, the Massachusetts effort was led, in part, by young lesbians and gays. Given a recent Harris poll indicating that there are roughly two million lesbian and gay adolescents in the United States, schools need to reach out to them to counter their isolation and high suicide rates. To do otherwise is to be guilty of malpractice.

Moves to be inclusive, though, have not gone unprotested by conservative religious forces and uninformed individuals. Rev. Lou Sheldon, head of the Traditional Values Coalition, opposed school-based counseling programs for lesbian and gay students in California.[17] In New York City, the Rainbow Curriculum, a program praised by educators, succumbed to conservative pressure led by Mary Cummins.[18] And when the Austin (Texas) Independent School District moved to include protection of lesbians and gays in its sexual harassment policy, the Rev. Charles Bullock, pastor of the Christ Memorial Independent Baptist Church, charged, "It is special rights for homosexuals—not equal rights."[19] Such protests are attempts to symbolically annihilate sexual minorities and are motivated by hate, misunderstanding, and intolerance. They fail to recognize the considerable good that an inclusive curriculum can have—not only for lesbian and gay students, but also for heterosexual students. Heterosexual students who study about homosexuality gain more comfort not only with homosexuality, but with their own sexual identity as well.[20]

Surviving the pain and isolation of high school, young lesbians and gays are heroes—each and every one of them—and now many are breaking their silence.

DAN, 19, Laramie, Wyoming

There are three major things that contribute to who I am, what decisions I make, and the personality that I have. These three things are my passion for cheerleading, my homosexuality, and my growing up Mormon. I have found that throughout my life, all of the joy, pain, happiness, and depression that I've been through can be attributed to the three. Of course, it's obvious that the biggest conflict exists between my being gay and also being Mormon.

I live in a small town in Wyoming called Laramie. For Wyoming, it is a metropolis; for a homosexual, it is a nightmare. The majority of the people who reside in Laramie, and in the whole state of Wyoming for that matter, are very conservative. Laramie is a college town and probably wouldn't exist if the university weren't here. Many of its residents are Mormon. These are the people whom I grew up around, and their ideas and morals influenced my childhood.

At quite an early age, I noticed that I was different from my heterosexual peers. In grade school, I never liked to do the traditional "boy" things. I never played basketball, touch football, or soccer. I always found myself playing with the girls—on the bars, four-square, hopscotch, and occasionally tetherball. I was always one of the smarter students and considered to be one of the "teacher's pets." These things went unchanged for the majority of elementary school. Only when I got older did I begin to realize that I didn't fit in.

At the end of my seventh-grade year, I tried out to be a cheerleader on the eighth-grade squad. On the first day of try-out practices, I was scared, excited, and afraid of what people would think. Cheerleading wasn't something that junior-high-school boys did in Wyoming. At first, my peers thought that I was just doing it as a joke. When they learned that I was serious about becoming a cheerleader, they didn't like it. The two weeks of try-out practices were hell, with taunts and jeers from my peers, but I made the cheerleading squad and was named one of the captains.

Over the summer, the squad went to cheerleading camp. The attention that I got from one of the instructors was wonderful. He saw that I had talent and potential and tried to nurture that during the week we were together. And I began to fall in love with him. That week I learned that cheerleading was for me, and so were men.

When school started again, I was as excited as the other cheerleaders about the first game. According to school policy, we were supposed to wear our cheerleading uniforms on game day to promote school spirit. That day became the longest day of my life.

I felt so many stares as I was walked to my locker before first period class. Accompanying those stares were jeers and rude comments. I've never heard the words *fag, fucking faggot,* and *queer* more than in that one day of my life. It hurt. I wanted to run home crying; but I also knew that was exactly what everyone wanted me to do, and I wasn't going to let them win that easily.

That evening at the game, a girl on the squad started saying how she couldn't wait until the game was over. Trying to be friendly, I asked if she had some exciting plans. She said, "You'll find out." Later, another girl on the squad told me that the football team was planning to tackle me and teach me a lesson.

I cheered loud for our team, and our team won the game. But when the other cheerleaders went out to congratulate them on their victory, I stood close to some parents. I wasn't going to give the team an opportunity to get me.

I went to church the next Sunday, and didn't find much comfort and support. For many in the Ward, it was their first realization that I was a cheerleader. The men seemed especially uncomfortable with it. I got the feeling that they felt it was an inappropriate activity for a boy, and I think it was then that I realized I was a disappointment to my father.

Where did I turn for comfort and support? There was no type of support for someone in my situation. I had nowhere to turn, but within myself and to the library. The university library had a large selection of books. It probably saved my life. When I doubted myself and wanted to know more about what I was and get another perspective about being gay, I read. I spent many, many hours in that library reading anything and everything I could find on the topic of homosexuality. Since I didn't have anyone to talk to, these books reaffirmed that I was not mentally ill, a freak of nature, or a pervert. I was not anything that the church told me I was. I was not the evil things my classmates called me at school. I was just different, and there wasn't anything wrong with having feelings for other men.

Everyone at school treated me as if I were dying of some contagious disease. This continued all the way through high school. Although the taunting and jeers eventually stopped in high school, my peers became more creative. While I cheered at football games, they threw pennies or drinks at me, sometimes inadvertently hitting another cheerleader. I still walked the halls of the high school in my cheerleading uniform every Friday we had a game, but I felt self-conscious about wearing it and began to think of it as an outer symbol of my sexuality. It was my silent way of saying, "*I am gay and proud.*"

I went through high school very much alone. I was not anyone's friend. Every weekend I stayed at home, unless I was working. By the time I graduated, I had experienced everything—discrimination, stereotyping, hatred, and threats. No one had the courage to reach out to me as a friend. But I learned early that I can't control the actions of others and that I should focus on myself and make the best of the circumstances I'm given.

After graduation from high school, I stayed in Laramie to attend the University of Wyoming. I'm glad that I stayed. Even though I wanted desperately to leave this town, if I had left I would never have met the people to whom I owe a great deal of thanks. In the fall, at the beginning of the semester, I got a job working as an office assistant for the University of Wyoming Graduate School.

Working there were Laura and Cindi. Laura had moved to Laramie in the fall to be with her fiance, Mark, who was going to graduate school. We decided that whenever I had some time, we would go to lunch. We talked at lunch about things we couldn't in the office. She told me about growing up in New York. She also told me about her homosexual friends. At the time, I didn't say much to Laura, but we went to lunch about once every two weeks after that. After about three friendly lunches together, we were driving back from the cafe and as we pulled into the parking space I told her that I was gay too. She just looked at me and smiled, and then she gave me a big hug. She offered the support I had needed for so long.

A few weeks later, Cindi asked Laura if I was gay, and Laura told her that I was. Cindi also became very supportive.

Laura and Cindi helped me overcome some of the heterosexual and Mormon hang-ups that I had with my sexuality. Through them I also met other young gay people who were gracious enough to take their time to help me find comfort with my sexual orientation.

I'm nineteen now and still have not told my family that I'm gay, although with everything that has happened in my life I don't see how they can *not* know. I want desperately to tell them. I'm tired of living a lie. Lying is the one thing that I've perfected over the years, as I'm sure most young homosexuals have. If there is one thing that I've learned from meeting other homosexuals who have come out to their parents already, it is that it is a long and difficult process.

I just want all homosexual youths out there to

know that there is hope. Feel good about your sexuality and understand that you are a unique individual.

DAVID, 19, Suitland, Maryland

I'm nineteen years old, and I'm gay.

It wasn't that long ago when being gay was something that I wouldn't have admitted. I mean, considering the homophobic society we live in, who would? Anyway, I probably didn't apply those words to myself until I was sixteen, a sophomore in high school, and found myself very much physically and emotionally attracted to a guy I went to school with. When I finally admitted it, I hated myself. Literally, I couldn't look myself in the mirror.

Everything I had heard about gays was bad. In our society, especially in our churches, many people equate being gay with being sinful, evil, and morally corrupt. I didn't want to be any of those things; but I also knew I was gay.

Fortunately, I had a few close friends with whom I could share my innermost thoughts and feelings. One of these was a former elementary-school classmate of mine who later moved to Arkansas. Throughout our high-school years, we exchanged correspondence; and as a result, I have a wonderfully detailed chronicle of coming to terms with my sexuality.

I would like to share with you some of these experiences, as I related them to my friend in Arkansas. For the sake of confidentiality, let's call her Mary.

June 1992

Dear Mary,

I must ask that this letter be kept private. I'm asking this because I don't know whether or not you share my letters with your sister. You see, I've decided to tell you that certain "thing" about me to which I alluded in my last letter. You've probably guessed it already, and if so, then this will just be a confirmation, and an effort to try to get you to understand. I guess there's no sense beating around the bush. You see the fact is . . . I'm gay. Yes, it's true; and yes, I'm sure.

As you know, I got shit for being "different" all through elementary school and still do in high school. All that time, I never once thought that I was gay (well, maybe, but I dismissed the thought immediately). Now I know I am, and I feel destined to live a life of persecution by society. It's a feeling that doesn't seem to go away. When I think about it, I don't even know if our friendship will change over this; I hope that it won't.

In elementary school, I had some sense that I was "different," but I couldn't quite put my finger on it. All through school, I was teased for acting effeminate and doing things that were considered "girlish," such as jumping rope. At first, I blamed my being gay on this verbal harassment. Everyone else said I was a *fag*, a queen, a *gay-gay*, so I thought I was, too. I went from hating *myself* to hating *them* for *making* me gay. This weird rationale came in spite of the fact that I had recognized a strong affectional attraction toward members of my own sex as far back as first grade.

In adolescence, I tried to cope with being gay through hard work and over achievement. I got straight As; I took several Advance Placement and Honors courses; I got high scores on my SATs; I was first-chair flutist in the band, a concert pianist, and an actor, singer, and dancer. I figured that if I made myself as good as possible, people would like me; and the question of being gay wouldn't come up.

It didn't happen that way. I was still the campus faggot.

August 1992

I'm scared, Mary. I don't want to go back to school. I start on Sept. 2nd. It's like I'll have to start lying to myself again, and pretending I'm someone else. At Spirit [a summer job on a dinner cruise ship working as a performing waiter, where David came in contact with other gays and found his own community], I didn't have to. And for a while, I started to believe that I was really eighteen [David lied about his age to get the job. He was seventeen.] and going off to college this fall. Gosh, I felt so free and uninhibited. But then reality slammed the door in my face. I've got to go back to that hell-hole again.

The negativity I encountered in high school was tenfold that in elementary school. This is probably due to the fact that there were no females, since I attended an all-male, Catholic high school. There weren't any girls with whom I could forge friendships and build support systems. Once again, I became the scapegoat. I had to be careful where I walked for fear of bearing the brunt of an embarrassing, derogatory slur. I couldn't even walk through the cafeteria in the morning to get to my homeroom, although this was by far the most direct route. If I did, I risked being taunted, laughed at, and made fun of; I risked physical gropes and having objects thrown at me.

You should be able to vaguely comprehend what a psychological strain it was for me to attend school. At the same time, I was trying to deal with family suspicions that I was gay.

October 1992

I came out to my mother! Well, I didn't voluntarily tell her; she asked me.

One morning at 6:00 A.M. (when I usually wake up to get ready for school, mind you!), she called me, crying, and said that she had been up all night and had something that she needed to ask me. I thought, OH, HELL!

"Judging from the previous conversations we've had," she said, "especially those about sex, I want to know if you are gay."

I could've died. I mean, this was it! Either I lied, thereby lying to myself and having to deal with that issue, or I 'fessed up. So I told her that after I answered her question, we would have to talk about it. Then I said, "Yes, I'm a gay male."

It was out! Well, she started crying again, and said that I had truly broken her heart. Then she hung up. I truly didn't know what to expect. I thought she was going to tell my dad, which I didn't want her to do, since he was the one whom I was living with. All through the day at school I was on pins and needles wondering what would happen. Would they throw me out? Would they still embrace me as their son? I didn't know.

That night, my mom and I eventually talked about it. Fortunately, she didn't tell my dad. She said she'd wait for me to tell him. In addition, she said she wanted to understand this and that she was going to find a support group (which she did: P-FLAG—Parents, Families, and Friends of Lesbians and Gays).

Later on that week, she met me at work and told me that she had come to give me a hug and to say that she would be there for me.

Six months later, I came out at school.

April 1993

I came out at school! I still can't believe I did it. It happened on April 1 at the senior retreat for the music students. I've just got a few more weeks of school left, and I know that it won't be all easy.

Three weeks later.

School has been a total hell! I really wasn't prepared for how hostile it actually would be. People are so ignorant. The faculty response has been generally supportive, but for the most part I get the feeling that they'd like to sweep me under the rug. As far as the students, it's been mixed. People are getting bolder now and are making derogatory remarks in the hallway and in the cafeteria. Someone even said that he hated me.

People have questions, but they usually don't ask me. They feel too threatened. That's the typical straight male response: thinking all gay men are out to get them. To tell you the truth, most of the guys at my high school are not desirable. Anyway, they don't talk to me; they talk to people they see me associating with. The two questions most frequently asked are: "What's it like to talk to him?" and "Does he—you know—try anything?" That says something about what they've learned at this school.

It really has been hell, Mary. I can't wait until June 4th.

In an attempt to counteract all that I was facing then and had faced throughout elementary and secondary school, I wrote an article titled "Coming Out at_____." It was an attempt to dispel some of the misconceptions and misinformation that so many people at my high school, as well as in society, held to be true. It was to be printed in the final issue of the school newspaper. Not surprisingly, the article was not printed at all; and neither the editor of the paper nor the principal of the school (who had authorized the censorship without even reading the article) had the courtesy to tell me. I found out upon reading the paper when it was distributed.

Because of this, my mother helped me print eight hundred copies of the article so I could distribute them myself the next day. Approximately three hundred of them had been distributed when the principal received word and summoned me to his office. He told me that if I persisted in distributing the article, I would not be allowed to participate in the graduation ceremony to be held the following week.

The following is an excerpt from my article:

Some would say that I'm courageous to openly face the thick fog of negativity that is not only very much concentrated in the hallways and classrooms of_____, but in society as a whole. Well, I can say it's not easy. Considering that my name is virtually synonymous with "faggot," that there are those who have openly stated that they hate me, that I constantly must be aware of those who may intend to do me physical harm, that the administration has practically enshrouded the topic of homosexuality in total silence, and that I am even seen by some as a threatening contagion to be leery of, you might think that I would crawl right back into the closet I just left. I can't. There's too much at stake. I don't simply demand tolerance of homosexuality, for tolerance implies some coercive force which one would not otherwise give; I demand respect, including the right to live my life and cultivate it just as any other person would do.

About one month after coming out in high school, I attempted suicide by taking an overdose of sleeping pills. Even if I had survived high school, there was still society to face. I decided that life was not worth living if I had to constantly fight and struggle with others who hate, loathe, and detest who I am. Everywhere I looked, whether it be on TV or in films, I was reminded of those hallways at school and found only validation and substantiation for my feelings of despair. Death became a viable alternative.

Fortunately, I wasn't successful. After a year of psychotherapy, I was able to start over and am rebuilding my life based on self-acceptance.

Dear Mary,
Trying to get my life back on track. But I'm taking it slow. Thank God for my therapist, and my mother's willingness to at least attempt to understand. And I really appreciate that. I'm really lucky to have a mom who is supportive of me.

Having survived the experiences I did throughout school, I not only have an obligation to myself, but also to others to speak out about the importance of broadening the scope of our schools' human-sexuality curricula, especially with respect to sexual-minority youths and their unique needs. It isn't about sexuality. It's about building self-esteem and self-worth. It's about providing a safe, nurturing environment for *all* youths to gain an education without fear of being degraded, derided, or physically harmed. It's about saving lives.

TERRA, 17, San Diego, California

"What is a gay kid to do? Life becomes disjointed, alien, a single path strewn with sharp shards of glass from banging against thousands of fun-house mirrors in a never-ending House of Horrors."

My friends and I sat giggling over the melodrama of this statement as we read an article on gay and lesbian suicide in the *Gay and Lesbian Times*. The three of us—James, Sarah, and I—knew all too well the struggles and depression involved with being a gay youth, but still thought this to be a little too dramatic. If we could only make being gay seem as commonplace as being straight, maybe the tragedies of gay bashings and suicide would not occur.

What I have found is that having good friends is a major factor in becoming comfortable with one's sexuality. I have known Sarah since I was a freshman in high school. She was a sophomore, but we became close friends because we were both on the tennis team. With my best friend Elizabeth and Sarah's best friend Jade, we had a close-knit group. We could discuss all of the typical teenage topics, such as love, school, and sex.

I had always noticed my tendency of being attracted to women. I became extremely self-conscious around other girls, thinking I might spend too much time admiring a girl's outfit or that I might turn my head a little too far around to peer at a woman walking down the street. I always wanted to share my curiosities with my friends, but I thought if I suppressed these feelings, they might go away. They didn't.

Finally, when Sarah was a senior, myself a junior, she came out to us. Of course, Elizabeth and Jade were fine with it, but it came as a surprise. Sarah had always pretended she was interested in boys so we wouldn't suspect. She was still very sensitive about the subject, so when Elizabeth asked her if she thought it had been her idolizing of James, a gay male friend of ours, or gay society that had caused her to be this way, she got very upset. I didn't blame Sarah for feeling frustrated by this, but I also understood, given the frequent religious charge of *recruitment*, why Elizabeth might ask.

A few days later, I told Sarah about my own interest in women. I declared myself *bisexual*, but in later time realized that I was more like three-fourths attracted to women. From then on, Sarah and I shared a special bond that we had never had before.

Since then, we have been attending Gay Youth Alliance together. Because I am only out to my friends, I don't have to deal with a lot of cruelty, as many others my age do. I'm waiting until I go to college to be "out." Many of the youths at Gay Youth Alliance have had serious problems with their families, friends, and classmates. What happens to James, for example, is not unusual for "suspected" or open lesbians and gays in high school. Students jeer at his way of walking, his attire, and his feminine voice. He has a right to be himself, but the other kids don't see it that way. They can be cruel, and James has attempted suicide because of the depression their treatment has caused.

At Gay Youth Alliance meetings we not only support one another, but it's also a nice way to meet other gays our own age. Because gay males always seem to outnumber the lesbians, I have made many close male friends there. Because our sexual orientations are different, we can have confusion-free friendships. We even went to prom together as a cover.

Once, to encourage more gays from our high school to come out, Sarah and I put an advertisement for Gay Youth Alliance in our school newspaper. It was so small that we thought no one would even see it, but we were wrong. There was a widespread reaction, proving to us that the youths of our generation are as insensitive as the older generation. In my math class, for instance, someone yelled in astonishment, "Look! A fag group."

When summer came, Sarah and I attended

the Gay Pride Parade for the first time. It was incredible. We had no idea that there were so many gays in San Diego. Families seemed so supportive. Sarah's mother even came to show her support. I was really happy to see that there were so many people like us around, but something was still missing: my family. I can never tell my mother that I am a lesbian while I am living at home. It would make my life too difficult. It feels really lonely not being able to share this side of my life with her.

Now that Sarah and James have graduated, I don't have any gay friends at school. Sarah's leaving for Berkeley, and she was my biggest support. I can now see why so many gay youths are lonely and frustrated. Though I know that gays and lesbians are everywhere, we are left to fend for ourselves in a very cold and close-minded society.

SHAWN, 18, San Diego, California

High school is a time when the immaturity of grade school and junior high is slowly relinquished and a place where new experiences, good and bad, continue to shape the mind and spirit. It's an environment where stereotypes and prejudice run rampant through the locker-lined halls and where a self-identified gay teenager can find hate, ignorance, and pain.

I am eighteen years old now, a freshman in college, and very secure about my sexuality as well as the other aspects of my personality that make me an individual. Being gay is a part of my life now, and I have accepted all that comes with it—the bad as well as the good times. But there

was a time when I was entering high school when confusion and fear and discomfort were the feelings that held the reins in my emotional life. I didn't know whom to trust, wasn't sure if I wanted to trust anyone, and hadn't yet met anyone in school like me. I had many gay friends outside of school, and my parents knew and were accepting. But not having any outlet in school, the place where I spent nearly half of my time, was a source of immense stress and uneasiness.

I found that as I became more comfortable with my sexuality, however, the thoughts and comments of other people ceased to hold importance in my life. My friends who accepted me for who I was became closer than ever before. Those whose ignorance and fear prevented them from accepting me, I did not waste my time with. I had reached a point in my life where I could do everything I needed for myself; independence was a way of life. All I needed from those around me was companionship, love, and respect. Anyone who could not give me these had no part in my life.

I graduated from high school with a good feeling about myself, my sexual orientation, and the people around me. What I also took with me was an expectation of what college would be like. Now that I am here, I see that my expectations were slightly different from the reality that greeted me. I left high school feeling that finally my life could begin for real, finally I would go to college and find a wonderful man to love and who would love me. The reality is that college is just another step in the learning and growing process that is ongoing in life. Meeting people is neither easier nor more difficult, just different. What I have found, though, is that if you love something enough, if you want something enough for yourself, it will happen, it will come to you, provided *you* make it happen. Life has an infinite array of experiences to offer. All one needs to attain dreams is a little perseverance and a lot of self-confidence.

ANTHONY, 19, Tucson, Arizona

Let me begin by introducing myself. My name is Anthony. I'm a nineteen-year-old Hispanic male. I am currently in my second year at the University of Arizona in Tucson, double-majoring in accounting and journalism. And, I am gay. Officially, I've been somewhat out for a year. I say "somewhat" because I'm only out to my friends, not to my par-

Anthony is on the left

ents or the rest of my family. So far, my life has not been complicated since I came out to my friends and myself, except for when I go back home to Sedona, Arizona. Those are the times when I must be both "butch and macho."

I went to high school in a conservative, rural town in northern Arizona. I know that one in every ten people is gay; with one thousand students in my high school, I knew I wasn't the only one. But I was the only one who did a lip sync in drag to Madonna's "Vogue," among other things. With this, I expected teasing by my peers. I was right about the teasing and sometimes it got bad, but I handled it well. I'm a very strong and "tough-skinned" person, so only a few things can discourage me, and name calling is not one of those things. I did realize, however, that I wasn't all that strong. To discourage the name calling, I took on a pseudo-girlfriend and tried to pass myself off as bisexual, thinking that would be a little better. Yeah, right! The name calling continued. Right before my senior year, I thought to myself, "Hey! What are you doing? You're trying to be something you aren't!" At this point, I knew that I was lying to myself and that lying was wrong, especially since my mom always told me to be myself and not something I'm not.

During my senior year, I changed. I realized that I was in fact gay, and not bisexual. I kept the girlfriend as a "cover," simply because I wasn't ready to admit this to anyone else yet. But the summer after my senior year, I finally dropped the girlfriend, who still thinks I'm bisexual, and started to find out about the real me. That led to my coming out to my friends and to where I am now.

As for learning about sexuality in high school, I could have done better in an adult bookstore. I think I would have learned more from that than what I was taught by the school. You would think that a school with one of the highest pregnancy rates in the state of Arizona would initiate a more accurate sex-education program, but they didn't, and still haven't. The parents of these students simply did not and do not want their "innocent" children taught about sexual intercourse, pregnancy, and AIDS in a public forum.

Luckily, during my sophomore year, I went to a different high school. There, a student was required to take a health class that also taught sex education during the semester. In this class, the instructors taught about heterosexuals and sex, but only a small amount of time was devoted to homosexuals and sex. Still, the instructors tried to do a good job educating us about the spread and prevention of AIDS in both the heterosexual and homosexual communities, as well as other sexual topics relating to both of these groups. While they were limited in what they could say about homosexuality, the instructors passed out pamphlets and other literature about homosexuals, gay sex, and AIDS. They did the best they could, given the situation, and it made all the difference in how I viewed myself.

At the school I graduated from, sex education wasn't taught until the senior year, and then only if the student's parents signed a permission slip. Compared to the other sex-education class I'd had, this class was a joke! Each time the instructor mentioned the words "penis," "vagina," "sexual intercourse," and any other words related to reproduction, she would whisper them! The most insulting and idiotic thing, in my opinion, was that the instructor could not utter the word "homosexuality," or anything pertaining to it, because the administration thought that the mention of such things would lead a person "to become gay." I consider myself lucky to have attended a more responsible school in tenth grade.

How are we, as eventually sexually active individuals, to know about safe sex, AIDS, and other related subjects, if school officials and parents think that it's too controversial to teach? Schools have a responsibility to the community, and that community includes homosexuals, even if school officials and parents refuse to acknowledge it.

MELANIE-JOY, 19, Coral Springs, Florida

I used to feel so
alone
at school.
No one else I knew,
male or female,
was gay.
Yesterday I saw
"Lesbian Love"
written on one of the walls
in the bathroom,
and I just wanted
to cry
with relief.

LESBIAN, GAY, AND BISEXUAL STUDENTS' BILL OF EDUCATIONAL RIGHTS

- The right to fair and accurate information about sexual orientation in textbooks and other classroom materials.
- The right to unbiased information about the historical and continuing contributions of lesbian, gay, and bisexual people in all subject areas, including art, literature, science, sports, and history/social studies.
- The right to positive role models, both in person and in the curriculum; the right to accurate information about themselves, free of negative judgment, and delivered by trained adults who not only inform lesbian, gay, and bisexual students, but affirm them.
- The right to attend schools free of verbal and physical harassment, where education, not survival, is the priority.
- The right to attend schools where respect and dignity for all students, including lesbian, gay, and bisexual students, is a standard set by the state Superintendent of Public Instruction, supported by state and local boards of education, and enforced by every district superintendent, principal, and school employee.
- The right to be included in all support programs that exist to help teenagers deal with the difficulties of adolescence.
- The right to legislators who guarantee and fight for their constitutional freedoms, rather than legislators who reinforce hatred and prejudice.
- The right to a heritage free of crippling self-hate and unchallenged discrimination.

—Project 21 (adapted from Project 10)

Nothing has been more volatile in recent years than the issue of homosexuality. In the past, it was either hidden from society at large or was misrepresented by wildly exaggerated images and false stereotypes. Since this hidden segment of society was unlikely to step forward to correct the inaccurate representations because of a realistic fear of reprisals, the negative images persisted. Silence brought a form of repression because society was willing to accept hearsay rather than judge people as individuals. In 1969, however, things changed.

In the early morning hours of June 28, a clash broke out between the police and patrons of the Stonewall Inn, a Greenwich Village tavern. In an era when "closeted" homosexuals were easy prey for police and ostracism was the price one paid for being labeled a homosexual, the patrons of the Stonewall Inn took to the streets and fought back against their police oppressors by hurling beer bottles and stones at them. Their response to the police harassment that summer evening was the beginning of today's gay civil-rights movement and the significance behind the annual gay-pride parades. The Stonewall Riots ushered in a tide of emerg-

> ## TALK RADIO HOSTS
>
> What is there to be proud of anyway—that they've perpetrated the most devastating plague since the Black Death . . . ?
>
> — Roger Hedgecock
> KSDO-Radio
> San Diego
>
> They don't want the same civil rights afforded to all other Americans. . . . They want special, preferential treatment accorded by law.
>
> —Rush Limbaugh

ing gay visibility—and the controversies and conflicts surrounding it.

At the very core of these controversies is religion, with conservative fundamentalist Christians often citing biblical scripture as a case *against* homosexuality. The Scriptures most often cited are Genesis 19:4-11, the story of Sodom; and Leviticus 18:22, that dictates that "man shalt not lie with mankind, as with womankind." These are the views expounded by Jerry Falwell, Pat Robertson, Donald Wildmon, Beverly LaHaye, James Dobson, Lou Sheldon, and others who selectively interpret the Bible in a literal sense and who use the issue of homosexuality to raise money and stir emotions. Grappling with these views are young people who have realized that the "difference" felt by them throughout their lives is an attraction to the same gender.

Young lesbians and gays don't intentionally set out to shock society by "becoming homosexual," nor does the realization of their sexual orientation turn them overnight into evil monsters. These are the same youngsters their parents, priests, ministers, and rabbis have always known and loved. Almost all of them aspire to have "normal" lives. Probably the majority of them who have grown up within a religion would wish to maintain that spiritual connection, if they were given a choice. But the views of most conservative fundamentalist religions force young lesbians and gays away from their spiritual houses, and they create great inner conflict in the process.

John J. McNeill, a Jesuit priest for nearly forty years, points out that biblical scripture is limited by history and culture.[1] Further, the passages used against homosexuality are "taken out of their context" and therefore clouded in interpretation. In nearly every mainline denomination, there are well-respected scriptural scholars "who believe that homosexual behavior is morally neutral [as neutral as heterosexuality] and who argue that the Bible does not speak clearly about the subject."[2] Hopscotch through the televised ministries, though, and you won't hear that message; you will hear only that homosexuality is evil and corrupt and damned, with televangelists pointing to the story of Sodom as proof.

> I was intrigued by Coach Bill McCartney at Colorado University, who quoted the thing from Leviticus, you know, that it is an abomination in the eyes of the Lord to—for a man to lie with another man. And I read a little further in Leviticus, and it said it is an abomination in the eyes of the Lord to touch the skin of a dead pig. And I thought, "Oh-oh, there goes football at CU."
>
> —Dr. Mel White

What was the sin of the Sodomites? Many scriptural scholars believe that the true sin of Sodom was *inhospitality*, and not homosexuality. Father Charles Curran, of Catholic University, grants "that the sin of the Sodomites 'does not necessarily involve a sexual connotation but could be interpreted as a violation of hospitality.'"[3] Dr. Mel White, himself a product of fundamentalist religious beliefs and a biblical scholar, believes that conservative fundamentalist religions have used a misinterpretation of Scripture for their own gain. His study of the story of Sodom concurs with Curran's: "The Sodomites were greedy, self-centered, and inhospitable."[4] At the very least, this suggests that biblical interpretations might be clouded by time and translation.

Dr. Martin Luther King, Jr., once said, "The church at times has preserved that which is immoral and unethical."[5] The Scriptures have been used to support slavery and deny the vote to women, just as they are used to condemn homosexuality. There is a tendency to isolate biblical verses and to use them for one's own purpose. Leviticus 18:22 is a case in point. While on the surface it appears to condemn homosexuality and make it punishable by death, it is a verse taken out of context. Within context, according to many respected biblical scholars, the condemnation appears to have more to do with idol worship than with homosexuality.[6] It was customary among some of Israel's neighbors to use temple prostitutes, both male and female, in certain religious rites. The condemnation of homosexual acts in Leviticus is actually a denunciation of the idolatrous activities male worshipers engaged in with male prostitutes provided by the temple. It has nothing to do with a condemnation of same-sex unions based on love and commitment.

Other sins in Leviticus are equally grave and include the following: Anyone who curses his father or mother shall be put to death (Lev. 20:9). Anyone who works on the Sabbath shall be put to death (Lev. 23:30). Even the *Fundamentalist Journal* admits that the Leviticus verses should not be taken literally today.[7] Who among us would kill a child for cursing a parent, or a sales clerk, police officer, or preacher for working on Sunday? Are these people guilty of serious sins for disobeying the writings in Leviticus? Why, then, are those verses which deal with homosexuality singled out for literal interpretation? To single out homosexuality is to be *selectively literal* and overlooks the very real possibility that the story upon which this condemnation is based, the story of Sodom, was inaccurately interpreted.

Misusing the Bible, though, is an old ruse. To align a position with Scripture is to give it sanction. Arguing a position counter to Scripture is to face severe condemnation. When Copernicus claimed that the sun was the center of our universe, there were calls by religious leaders for him to be silenced. When Galileo argued the Copernican position, the pope called Galileo a heretic and placed him under arrest. Both Copernicus and Galileo were victims of literal interpretations of Scripture. The Scriptures told their critics that the sun rises and sets (Ecclesiastes 1:5) and that the earth cannot be moved (Psalm 93). In 1992, three centuries after the fact, Pope John Paul II finally admitted that the church had been wrong. It had misused the Bible to condemn Copernicus and Galileo and to support a view of the universe that science has proven incorrect.[8]

Because they are historical texts, biblical scriptures weren't written with an understanding of homosexuality in terms of modern biological science. Any interpretation of them must be taken with historical and scientific limitations in mind. In biblical times, homo-sexuality wasn't understood as an involuntary *orientation*. While the causes of homosexuality aren't completely understood today, there is a growing body of evidence that points to biological factors. A study reported in the July 1993 issue of *Science* indicates that it is genetically inherited, the same way an individual inherits hair color and eye color.[9] It's a natural gift. But religious thinking changes slowly. Perhaps, as it was with Copernicus and Galileo, religious thinking will in time change its position on homosexuality, and lesbians and gays will be welcomed as equals into mainstream congregations.

Until religious thinking does change, however, fundamental evangelists who preach against homosexuality to raise money for their ministries and homophobic talk show hosts who do the same to drive up program ratings will bear the guilt of the hatred and hostility directed toward lesbians and gays. It is ironic that these were the same tactics used by Hitler and the Nazi Third Reich to marginalize minorities, including gays, to amass support for their eventual rise to power. Spoken words are powerful, and they can do considerable good—or harm. Hitler's speeches moved a nation to annihilate millions of Jews and some 220,000 homosexuals—the second largest group after the Jews—and he ever positioned himself as working on the side of the Lord. Before the National Republican Convention in 1992, Patrick Buchanan likened the conservative Christian movement to a Holy War. How many more lesbian and gay lives will be lost before these orators stop misusing religion and the Scriptures for their own financial and political gain and as justification for hate?

> I know that men are won over less by the written word than the spoken word, that every great movement on this earth owes its growth to great orators . . . and not to writers.
>
> —Adolf Hitler

People with AIDS want everyone to feel sorry for them. But God sent this plague and only He can take it away.

Nathan Giddings
Bishop
Old Ship of Zion
Church, Philadelphia

As the verbal assault on homosexuals from conservative Christians has grown, so have the number of physical assaults. When Acquired Immune Deficiency Syndrome (AIDS) entered the picture, it was incorrectly viewed as a "gay disease," and religious conservatives seized the opportunity to label it "God's retribution for sinful living." It was like adding the proverbial fat to the fire. The number of physical assaults against lesbian and gay individuals, and those perceived to be lesbian and gay, increased dramatically. Many believe that AIDS and the verbal barrage from religious conservatives gave "homophobic people 'permission' to express it."[10] Most religious conservatives pointed the finger of blame. One church, led by Bishop Nathan Giddings, even banned AIDS victims and homosexuals from entering its doors. As conservative religious leaders turned their backs on those in need, the lesbian and gay communities organized to assist victims and to educate themselves about the disease's spread. As a consequence, adults modified their sexual behaviors, but it is clear from recent studies that educational programs failed to reach many young people.

As of 1991, the Centers for Disease Control and Prevention reported that AIDS had become the nation's tenth leading killer of all Americans. Among younger people, though, it was the third major cause of death.[11] More than a decade into the disease, many youths are repeating the pre-AIDS sexual patterns In part, this is because many religious conservatives don't want schools to educate young people about sex—and definitely not about homo-sex. But they don't deserve all the blame. Young people have always been prone to a feeling of immortality. Paul A. Paroski, Jr., a pediatrician who has worked with gay and bisexual teens in New York City, describes their reaction to AIDS as a kind of denial: "The AIDS crisis does not apply to them, but only to older gay men."[12]

There are other factors, as well. The Center for AIDS Prevention Studies (CAPS), of the University of California at San Francisco, says that young gays feel so isolated and uncared for that they see little reason to protect themselves. One respondent to a CAPS survey wrote, "It seems like nobody cares if I die anyway."[13] Correspondingly, others are so eager to feel loved that they will risk anything—even AIDS. Eric Ciasullo, an AIDS educator with Lavender Youth Recreation and Information Center (LYRIC) of San Francisco, says that hostile school environments, abusive parents and siblings, gangs, and dismal employment prospects make it difficult for youths to place AIDS high on their list of priorities. Also, many have simply adopted a fatalistic attitude. "A lot of younger guys," Ciasullo says, "just think they're bound to get infected, so why bother going to all the trouble to practice safe sex?"[14] Neither are lesbians and gays without blame. In a society that worships youth and shuns older individuals—and this is, unfortunately, *very* true in the homosexual community—many young people see risky behavior as one way to avoid growing old, to avoid rejection.[15]

Another issue has arisen in the wake of increased gay visibility, of outspoken religious conservatives, and of AIDS: civil rights. Numerous reports have shown a

SEX AND AIDS

ABSTINENCE is the only 100% sure way not to get AIDS or other sexually transmitted diseases.

"Safe" sex includes:
Talking
Holding
Hugging
Kissing
Massage
Masturbation (solo)

Also considered "safe":
Masturbation (mutual)
Be certain that you or your partner do not have any open wounds that may come into contact with bodily fluids.

Vaginal, anal, and oral sex *with a latex condom.*
With the condom, use a water-based lubricant that contains nonoxynol-9. Be aware that condoms are not 100% effective; they can tear. For added protection, use two.

Risky behavior includes:
- Vaginal, anal, and oral sex *without a latex condom.*
- Any exchange of bodily fluids (blood, semen, and vaginal secretions).
- Sex while intoxicated or "high."
- Sharing needles if you do drugs.

steady pattern of discrimination against lesbians and gay men in several areas, including employment, public accommodations, housing, health care, parenting, and education. One report indicated that one-quarter of the employers surveyed said that they would not promote someone they perceived to be homosexual; another indicated that 50 percent of employment recruiters would screen out job applicants whom they suspected were lesbian or gay.[16] Some might ask, "What's wrong with that?" The only response to that question is another question: Would it be fair to withhold a promotion or deny employment to a perfectly capable person who had freckles simply because the employer held a bias against people with freckles? Most people would agree that such an arbitrary action based on a personal whim has no place in a society built upon equality, mutual respect, and fairness.

In an effort to gain a modicum of security, lesbians and gays have argued loud and hard for legal protection against such unfair discrimination. If an African-American or a woman were to be fired from a job because of race or gender, there is legal recourse that the individual can pursue. For a lesbian or gay man, though, fired because of sexual orientation, there is no protection—unless one happens to live in one of a handful of communities and states that have added "sexual-orientation" clauses to their civil-rights statutes.

There are some who wish not to extend civil rights to homosexuals. Attempts—like Colorado's Amendment Two—to deny equality to lesbians and gays are

> I talked to my real-life kids, and I said, "If you tell me you're gay, I plan to be really, really bored. If you tell me you're going to be a Republican, I shall be shocked."
>
> —Roseanne Barr

proliferating. They argue that what lesbians and gays want are *special rights*. They insist, against overwhelming evidence to the contrary, that the rights of homosexuals aren't threatened. They say that what homosexuals want is permission to live *an immoral lifestyle*, again injecting religion and the Scriptures to sway public opinion. Religious conservatives are fighting hard and using their considerable financial resources to deny lesbians and gays equal protection under the law, and Pope John Paul II, among others, is encouraging them to do so.

Many young lesbians and gays are stepping into the arena and picking up the struggle to fight prejudice and misinformation. They're telling conservative religious leaders that they will not be labeled *immoral* and *evil*, as the object of love does not dictate personal character. They're telling the Falwells and Sheldons of the world that they are not destroyers of families, for each and every one of them is part of one—and more and more families are turning their backs on the vitriolic messages of religious conservatives to support and love their lesbian and gay children. Young people are organizing themselves in out-reach programs to inform their queer peers about responsible behavior, and they're encouraging each other to be honest with themselves. And yes, they have adopted the word *queer*, and apply it to themselves with pride—a slap in the face to those who would use the word as a slur.

While not every young homosexual is able to stand up and be counted because there is considerable ignorance in the world to work against, significant numbers of lesbian and gay teens are saying to the critics, "You don't know me." They are standing up to their straight peers to shatter old images and myths. They're demanding a place at the table—for themselves and for those not yet able to come to the table.

While adults, straight and gay alike, speak out on issues that have a direct impact on today's young lesbians and gays, these youths are thoughtful themselves and quite capable of voicing their own opinions.

RICA, 20, Oberlin, Ohio

I was born into a happy home with two parents. Although it was a liberal, Jewish family, I was educated in a religious Hebrew day school. To be fair, the school that I attended for nine years (K-8) was very open for a Jewish day school. Students who attended it came from many different backgrounds. And these children were accepted by all; it was a bicultural family.

I was taught that acceptance is a virtue, that kindness, lending help, and inclusion are fundamental to Judaism. A "good Jew" was a good person. Though religious practices were important, morality was equally, if not more, important. We were taught "do not do unto others as you would not have them do unto you."

I went onto Westchester Hebrew High School, an orthodox Hebrew high school. Right off the bat, I was the odd one out. I was not orthodox. I had to take the train in from an hour away. I was the most liberal thinker in the school. And I was rather outspoken as a freshman. I would not be surprised if people stereotyped me as a lesbian because of my firm, liberal beliefs.

I was looked down upon by peers because I was offended by the misogynistic behavior of several teachers. It was common for them to say, "You girls won't understand this, but the men will." Women were not at all taken seriously, especially in religious and ethics classes. Most people were silent about it. But because of the firm beliefs I had about social action, which had been instilled by my parents and previous school, I could not remain silent. When the subject of homosexuality came up, I especially could not allow the insults to go unprotested.

I will NEVER forget the day that a rabbi said, "We should stick all the chinks, niggers, femi-nazi dykes and fags [said feigning a limp wrist] into a big room and nuke them!" This prompted the class to join in a cheer: "Nuke 'em!" Not only was this said by a rabbi, but by a man who was teaching a class on ethics. That day I walked out of class, but not before telling him how disgusted I was at his racist, homophobic remarks and actions. I think that was also the day that I realized how different I was from them. I was bisexual.

Coming to accept my sexuality was difficult enough before, but I now knew what territory I was in. I was not welcome by the mainstream of this small school. Sex and interactions between men and women were taboo enough, homosexuality and bisexuality were wicked. I was in hostile territory.

There is a loop-hole, one that I learned in that institution, ironically enough. Many people say that according to the Torah, homosexual activity is prohibited. Well, yes and no. There is a law that states, "No man shall lie with another man as he does with a woman." But this statement is open to interpretation. On face value, it seems to be an antigay law. At the time that the Torah and laws were being interpreted, though, homosexual activity was associated with worship among certain tribes. Some theologians view the prohibition of homosexuality as, in fact, a strike against their pagan worship. As an act of love, homosexuality is not prohibited. There are those who debate this; but even given that there is a prohibition, it is against men lying with men. There is no prohibition against women lying with women. In hindsight, had I been open enough and daring enough, I would have argued that according to the Torah there is nothing wrong about women being with women. But hindsight is 20/20.

For me, at this stage in my life, I don't think that I can engage in same-sex activity. This is not because I am not bisexual and attracted to women. I am, indeed. But having been in such a hostile environment, one could say I am scarred.

SUSAN, 16, San Diego, California

I am happy to say that I have no horrendous experiences to report when it comes to my being lesbian and religiously active. As a young child, I had little experience with organized religion. I was occasionally required to join my grandparents at their small-town church in the Midwest, but that was relatively harmless and they never cared to tell their tots about sexual "deviants," as I have heard members of various Christian sects designate those of my sexual identity. I made the decision in junior high that I neither believed in their

God, nor in the Catholic one predominant in town, so I announced my atheism and left it at that for some time. I was considered "weird" for that conviction, but there were no other options at the time.

I wouldn't describe my youth as overly joyous, but neither was it dreadful. I managed to avoid anything more severe than mild despair and occasional suicidal thoughts. Fortunately, I did not begin to discover my lesbianism until after my parents divorced and I moved in with my mother in San Diego, California. I'm sure I would have needed a higher power to appeal to if I'd realized it in small-town Ohio.

The first Sunday I was in California, my mom dragged me to her church. This is probably one of the best moves she's ever made; it's certainly the one I thank her for most. (Any of you out there who remain heathen and happy, don't worry. The following is not a salvation story.) It was there at the First Unitarian Church that I found a third or fourth boyfriend who adored me, but whom I just couldn't love *that way*. I'd had *that* experience before, but until I learned that there was such a thing as homosexuality, I'd just thought that I was too young or had the wrong boy or just wasn't good enough to fall in love.

The big difference was that I could finally pinpoint a reason why I wasn't totally enthralled with boys. At the beginning of my sophomore year, I met a junior named Sarah and developed the biggest crush I'd ever had. This was, of course, very confusing at first. Like many gays and lesbians (and heterosexuals, for that matter) who start life in small towns or with conservative or ignorant parents and teachers, there was no discussion of homosexuality when it came time for my birds-and-bees lecture; my only exposure to the word "lesbian" was as a nasty name you got called on the playground. However, the church came to my rescue. Every other spring, the Unitarian Church offered a course for junior and senior-high students called "About Your Sexuality." I enrolled and was quickly granted not only a name for my attraction, but also the support of my peers and advisers when I said I thought I might be bisexual. With that support came the security of discovering you're not alone in the world.

I've always found the Unitarian Universalist (UU) community to be a welcoming place for me, a family that never judges me but encourages me to be who I am. I am not the only UU lesbian who's had this experience. In fact, nearly every large UU congregation in the country has some sort of support group or social/political organization for gay people in the church and in the community at large. In 1994, the San Diego church dedicated a Sunday sermon to "Affirming the Inherent Worth and Dignity of All People," especially that of gays, lesbians, and bisexuals. The following weekend, I marched with my church friends, gay and "non-gay," in the San Diego Gay Pride Parade. With over one hundred members, we made up the largest contingent in the parade. This was not a publicity stunt to increase membership, nor was it followed by a ripple of dissention from persons in the church wishing to distance themselves from anything bearing the name "gay." The Gay/Lesbian Outreach (GLO) group sets up a table during fellowship hour every single Sunday, and they are always greeted warmly by passersby and visitors seeking information. I have experienced no hostility there toward those of us who identify ourselves as gay, lesbian, or bisexual, nor have I seen it from any of us toward the heterosexual members of the congregation.

My intention with this essay is not to advertise for my denomination, and certainly not to convert anyone. All I'm trying to do is let young gays and lesbians experiencing the situation I was in five years ago—stranded in a small, conservative town, turned off by the two religions I'd ever been exposed to, and suicidal because I saw no other way out—know that there is something else out there. There are organized groups of real people, Unitarian Universalist and otherwise, who will lend support regardless of your sexual orientation, race, age, background, or anything else.

I realize that not everyone reading this has immediate access to such an institution or a parent who's about to let them attend its meetings. I also realize that not everyone wishes to take up a spiritual calling or to associate closely with those who have. My point is intended for those who have been spiritually disillusioned and discouraged by their own church. Not all religious groups condemn you for whom you love. There is an excellent chance that among the hundreds of denominations and thousands of congregations in the United States some will be willing to listen, to accept you for yourself, and to tell you the sorts of things you need and want to hear. If you can't seem to find any of them, try your local library or just continue reading this book for resources. Above all, don't give up. Don't compromise who you are. Be honest with yourself, and eventually you'll find an organization like the Unitarian Universalist Church that's ready to extend its love to you.

CURTIS, 21, Los Angeles, California

I remember as a child my first impressions of sex. I would hear older children talking about sex or see photographs of nude women my stepfather kept hidden in the basement or my friends' fathers kept hidden in their basements. I remember that talking about sex or listening to other people talk about sex stirred something remotely frightening and exciting inside me. At that time, sex was an oddly fascinating, mysterious, unbelievable, and slightly ridiculous act. My realization that this was one of life's perks was my first awareness of my humanness. I looked forward to the days when I could express myself sexually, and I believed that it would change my life. At a time in my life when everything seemed out of reach, I would fantasize about the day I would be old enough to participate in this thing called "sex."

I first read about "safe sex" in a newspaper article very soon after I had started having sex. My first reaction to safe sex was similar to my first reaction to the idea of sex itself. "What the hell is safe sex? Sex through plastic? You mean no skin?"

A new disease called Acquired Immune Deficiency Syndrome (AIDS), had been discovered, and it weakened the body's immune system. It was a lethal disease that had no cure and was transmitted during sex. The reality of this seemed too arcane to believe. This new disease, AIDS, frightened and fascinated me. It had affected primarily gay men and intravenous drug users in this country, but was already at epidemic proportions in Africa and Haiti.

Okay, I was a young adult, out from under parental guidance and living on my own for the first time in a college town with a bunch of similarly post-pubescent creatures exploding with sexual energy. It was a time of great freedom and sexual expression for us. Only now, there was this new threat looming on the horizon. Sex began to take on a more intimidating air. Although my peers didn't seem too alarmed, I could see that sex was not going to be what it had promised to be—at least not for me. Just as I was ready to explore my sexuality, sex was beginning to take on new limitations.

As the years marched on, this new disease did the same. I was confounded by the semi-casual attitude toward this new terror. I believed that AIDS would be remedied or at least seriously addressed, but there didn't seem to be any sense of urgency about AIDS by the government or the average American citizen. Since this disease affected primarily gay men and intravenous drug users in the Western world, could our government believe that AIDS wasn't a national health priority? Could Middle America believe that, as Pat Buchanan stated, AIDS was Nature's retribution for homosexuality? And even if the consensus was that AIDS is not my problem, could your average American believe that it never would be?

The medical community seemed to be alarmed, but instead of focusing its resources on solutions to the AIDS problem, it was forced to concern itself with alerting the country to the potential of this new disease. Due in part to the fact that we were powerless against this new disease, the politics of AIDS became more important than the disease itself. The only way of combating AIDS was in the education of how to prevent it from spreading.

Soon after graduating from college, I moved to San Francisco where AIDS was a part of everyday life. I found myself in a big city with billboards and bus stops plastered with safe sex and AIDS education ads. Slowly, AIDS came into the American mainstream consciousness. I began to see TV commercials telling me to "Get the Facts," and AIDS-prevention programs were everywhere. Schools began distributing condoms and information on how to use them. Famous people began contracting AIDS, and politicians could no longer avoid this taboo health-crisis issue. A new era crept up on America. Our society started to acknowledge something that struck at our biggest fears: A disease that was transmitted sexually forced us to confront our sexuality, and its lethality forced us to confront our mortality.

A decade since the outbreak of AIDS in this country, we know much more about this disease. We have extensive AIDS education available and several drugs that slow the process of the HIV virus, believed to be responsible for AIDS. But we still know very little about this mysterious syndrome. Unsafe sex among adolescents and twenty-somethings is rampant and due to the lengthy incubation period for HIV, the potential for infection is astounding. Assigned risk for certain sex acts can range from low to very high, depending on the source. And HIV is getting more infectious. There are many different strains of the disease and some are undetectable by standard HIV tests. The game of love and sex has become quite complicated.

We now live in a time of fear and great uncertainty concerning sex. Gone are the days of free love and casual sex, or they should be. Our concerns now are whether we are going to live through sex, not how to find it. Much has changed regarding sex since I was a child. Expressing myself sexually could change my life as I once envisioned, but not in any way I could have predicted. What would sex be like without the threat of AIDS? I can only wonder.

SCOTT, 21, Branchville, New Jersey

No matter what the outcome, the campaign tactics were similar in both states. Both the Oregon Citizens' Alliance (OCA) and Coloradans for Family Values (CFV), organizations purporting to stand up for all that is right and good in the world, operated under the rallying cry of "No Special Rights!" This seemingly simple phrase has been the crux of the recent antigay movement, particularly among Christian fundamentalists. These organizations, and others, convinced uninformed people that gays were pushing for special rights and trying to subvert their wholesome American goodness. They argued that, as citizens, gays already had the same rights as everyone else, so by pushing for "gay-rights" bills they must certainly be asking for "special" rights, something over and above what they allegedly were already enjoying.

This is not the case. Heterosexuals can be legally married. They are legally entitled to spousal benefits. Partners of straights are usually treated as "family" by hospitals, jails, government agencies, and others who allow visitation or privileges to family and no others. Heterosexuals can-

not be evicted or fired simply because they are heterosexual. Heterosexual couples engaging in most forms of consensual sex are not breaking the law. Heterosexuals generally need not worry about being beaten or killed simply because they are straight.

In most of the United States, gays do not enjoy these privileges. Only some companies recognize "spousal equivalents" and award benefits and other privileges given to straight couples. Only eight states currently have laws protecting gays from discrimination in housing and employment. Several states still have laws prohibiting sodomy, which technically includes heterosexual oral and anal sex, but the laws are generally only applied to gays. Gay-bashing is common; people are beaten, killed, and persecuted because of their sexual orientation.

Many right-wing radicals, particularly the Christian fundamentalists, would have voters believe that gays are asking for something special. To them, the equality gays ask for is a "special right." Freedom from discrimination is a "special privilege." AIDS, which is not by a long shot a "gay disease," is God's punishment, well deserved. Gays are out to steal their children, to rape and molest innocents, to push their liberal agenda through, to wipe the goodness out of the lives of good Christians. They demonize gays, focusing on drag queens, Dykes on Bykes, leather queens, and other subsets which enrich the gay community. They spread their misinformation, bringing the uninformed to their side. Most of the American people don't know any gays, or don't know it if they do. The only images they have of gays are the "freaks" they see on TV, sent to their sets with a strong antigay message from the fundamentalists.

The right is phenomenally organized, and has more than sufficient funds from donations sent by people anxious to support good Christian causes—a ticket into heaven. They make videotapes, print pamphlets, and send mailings. They have a firm grassroots organization that gay organizations can only begin to counter. Gays need to spread the truth, try to match every antigay pamphlet with a positive one, and present positive images.

Too many gay youths attempt suicide. Even one attempt is too many. Hate and misinformation are perpetuated in homes, churches, and schools; young people hear that gay is bad and don't hear any different, so it must be true. It's not. They hear people tell fag jokes, see people laugh at them, and think that the jokes must be right and they must be wrong. They're not. It's okay to be gay; it's not "abnormal" or "wrong." More and more celebrities are coming out and being positive gay role models, people for youths to look at and say, "They're gay and they're okay. I'm okay, too."

The antigay message is especially true in rural areas. I grew up in rural New Jersey, a mostly-white, unwaveringly Republican area. I have fortunately not seen open hostility toward gays in the area, but I do know that most people with whom I went to high school would be very uncomfortable with my homosexuality. I didn't come out until I had left the area for college, and I've been fortunate to attend a gay-friendly school. I do believe, however, that if I came out to the people I know in rural New Jersey, their opinion of me would change. People who have known me for years, know who I am and what I'm about, but not that I'm gay, would probably feel differently about me simply because of my sexual orientation. This is wrong, terribly wrong, and it needs to change.

Gays are slowly gaining acceptance by countering the right's misinformation campaigns. But this is a slow, painstaking effort. Until we live in a world where the antigay messages are gone and gay youths no longer feel as if they're wrong, as if the dominant heterosexuality of society is crushing them, we need to keep working. We need to be sure to reach every young gay person we can and let them know that being gay is all right and that they are good people, no matter what others might say.

If you are a lesbian or gay youth, or you have a friend who might be lesbian or gay, the following resources may be helpful to you. I've tried to include as many different types of resources as possible because I understand that not everybody has the same comfort zone. Some people might find it intimidating to walk into a lesbian and gay social-service agency, but be at ease in a bookstore or library. Because I also know that many lesbian and gay youths transit the electronic highway with expert skill, I've included E-mail addresses when they were available.

Most of all, I want lesbian and gay youths to know that you are not alone. I hope this book and the following resources will provide you with a foundation for self-acceptance, self-worth, and self-love.

MAGAZINES

InsideOut
PO Box 460268
San Francisco, CA 94146-0268
Phone: 415/487-6870

E-mail:
insideout@igc.apc.org
insideout2@aol.com

OUT
PO Box 1935
Marion, OH 43306-2035
Phone: 800/669-1002
E-mail: outmag@aol.com

OutYouth Newsmagazine
208 West 13th Street
New York, NY 10011

Y.O.U.T.H.
PO Box 34215
Washington, DC 20043
Phone: 202/234-3562

SOCIAL SERVICE AGENCIES

CANADA

British Columbia
Gay & Lesbian Center
1170 Bute Street
Vancouver, V6E 1Z6
Phone: 604/684-6869

LGB Youth Program
Suite 300
65 Wellesley Street East
Toronto, M4Y 1G7
Phone 416/924-2930

Ontario
LGB Youth of Toronto
519 Church Street
Toronto, M4Y 2C9
Phone: 416/971-LGYT

UNITED STATES

Alabama
Gay/Lesbian
Information Line
Lambda Inc.
PO Box 55913
Birmingham, 35255
Phone: 205/326-8600

Lambda Resource
Center
516 S. 27th Street
Birmingham
Phone: 205/326-8600

MALAGA
PO Box 40326
Mobile, 36640
Phone: 205/433-3245

Lambda Triangle
Center
609 Hull Street
PO Box 40326
Montgomery, 36101
205/834-0018

Alaska

Gay Helpline Identity, Inc.
PO Box 200070
Anchorage, 99520
907/258-4777

3E Alaska Gay/Lesbian Alliance
PO Box 211371
Auke Bay, 99821
907/586-4297

Arizona

Gay & Lesbian
Community Center
PO Box 183
Flagstaff, 86002
602/526-6098

Lesbian/Gay
Community Switchboard
PO Box 16423
Phoenix, 85011
602/234-2752

Information & Referral Service
2555 East 1st Street, #107
Tucson, 85716
602/881-1794

Wingspan
422 North 4th Avenue
Tucson, 85705
602/624-1779

Arkansas

Gay & Lesbian Task Force
Switchboard
PO Box 45053
Little Rock, 72214
501/666-3340 (Little Rock)
800/448-8305 (Statewide)

California

Pacific Center Switchboard
2712 Telegraph Avenue
Berkeley, 94705
Phone: 415/548-8283
415/841-6224

Gay & Lesbian Resources
PO Box 3480
Camarillo, 93011
Phone: 805/389-1530

Stonewall Alliance
PO Box 8855
Chico, 95927

Lambda Youth Network
PO Box 7911
Culver City, 90233
Phone: 310/821-1139
E-mail. lambdayn@aol.com

Gay United Services, Inc.
Box 4640
Fresno, 93744
209/268-3541

Gay/Lesbian
Community Services
12832 Garden Grove
Boulevard, #A
Garden Grove, 92643
Phone: 714/534-0862
Hotline: 714/534-3261
TDD: 714/534-3441

EAGLES Center (high school)
7051 Santa Monica Boulevard
Hollywood, 90038
Phone: 213/957-0348

Laguna Outreach
PO Box 1701
Laguna Beach, 92652
Phone: 714/472-8807

ONE
The Center
2917 East 4th Street
Long Beach, 90814
Phone: 310/434-4455

Community Services Center
1213 North Highland
Avenue
Los Angeles, 90038
Phone: 213/464-7400
TDD: 213/464-0029

Project 10
Fairfax High School
7850 Melrose
Los Angeles, 90046
Phone: 213/651-5200 ext.
244

Youth Outreach
1625 North Hudson Avenue
Los Angeles, 90028
Phone: 213/993-7451

Project Teens
One East Olive Avenue
Redlands, 92373
909/335-2005

South Bay Lesbian/Gay
Community Center
PO Box 2777
Redondo Beach, 90278
Phone: 213/379-2850

Lambda Community Center
PO Box 163654
1931 L Street
Sacramento, 95816
Phone: 916/442-0187

Rainbow's End
1000 Sir Francis Boulevard
Room 10
San Anselmo, 94960
Phone: 415/457-3523

Gay & Lesbian Center
PO Box 6333
San Bernardino, 92412
Phone: 714/824-7618

The Center
3916 Normal Street
San Diego, 92103
Phone: 619/692-GAYS
Youth: 619/233-9309

Lesbian & Gay Historical
Society
4545 Park Boulevard
San Diego, 92103
Phone: 619/260-1522

Gay Area Youth Switchboard
Box 846
San Francisco, 94101
Phone: 415/386-GAYS

LYRIC
(Lavender Youth Rec.
Center)
3543 18th Street, Apt. 31
San Francisco, 94110
Phone: 415/703-6150
Helpline: 800/246-PRIDE

Billy De Frank Community
Center
175 Stockton Avenue
San Jose, 95126
Phone: 408/293-4525

Youth Outreach
Gay & Lesbian Resource
Center
126 East Haley Street
Santa Barbara, 93101
Phone: 805/963-3636

Lesbian & Gay Community
Center
1332 Commerce Lane
PO Box 8280
Santa Cruz, 95061
Phone: 408/425-LGCC

Helpline
Box 1203
Santa Rosa, 95402
Phone: 707/544-HELP

Lesbian/Gay Bisexual
Community Center
Santa Teresa Street, near
Tresidder Memorial Union
Box 8265
Stanford, 94309
Phone: 415/725-4222

Gay and Lesbian Adolescent
Social Services (GLASS)
650 North Robertson
Boulevard
Suite A
West Hollywood, 90069
310/358-8727

Colorado
Gay & Lesbian Community
PO Box 3143
Aspen, 81612
Phone: 303/925-9249

Pikes Peak Gay/Lesbian
Community Center
PO Box 574
Colorado Springs, 80901
Help Line: 719/471-4429

Gay & Lesbian Association
PO Box 244
Delta, 81416
Phone: 303/874-5510

Community Center of Colo.
1245 East Colfax #125
Denver, 80218
Help Line: 303/837-1598

Gay & Lesbian Task Force
PO Box 18632
Denver, 80218
Phone: 303/830-2981

Youth Services Program
PO Drawer 18-E
Denver, 80218
Phone: 303/831-6268
Helpline: 303/324-GAYS

Connecticut
Danbury, 06810
Helpline: 203/426-4922

Gay, Lesbian & Bisexual
Community Center
1841 Broad Street
Hartford, 06114
Phone: 203/724-5524

BGLAD4YOUTH
c/o AIDS Project New
Haven
PO Box 636
New Haven, 06503
Phone: 203/624-0947

Info. Line of Southeast CT
74 West Main Street
Norwich, 06360
Phone: 203/886-0516

Gay & Lesbian Guideline
Stamford, 06905
Phone: 203/327-0767

Delaware
Gay & Lesbian Alliance
800 West Street
Wilmington, 19801
Phone: 302/655-5280
Hotline: 800/292-0429

District of Columbia
Gay & Lesbian Hotline
Whitman-Walker Clinic
1407 South Street, NW
Washington DC, 20009
Phone: 202/833-3234
Spanish: 202/332-2192

SMYAL
(Sexual Minority Youth
Assistance League)
333½ Pennsylvania Avenue,
SE
Washington DC, 20003
Phone: 202/546-5911

Florida
Center One
Fort Lauderdale, 33310
Phone: 305/485-7415

Support, Inc.
Fort Myers, 33902
Helpline: 813/275 1400

Gay Switchboard
Gainesville
Phone: 904/332-0700

Polk Gay/Lesbian Alliance
Lakeland, 33802
Phone: 813/682-4652

Community Hotline
Lambda Passages
Miami, 33138
Phone: 305/759-3661

Switchboard of Miami
Miami, 33130
Phone: 305/358-HELP

Gay/Lesbian Community
Services
750 West Colonial Drive
Orlando, 32853
Phone: 407/843-4297
Hotline: 407/649-8615

The Line
St. Petersburg, 33733
Phone: 813/586-4297

Gay & Lesbian Alliance
Sarasota, 34277
Phone: 813/365-4669

Women's Info. Line
1704 Thomasville Road, #113
Tallahassee, 32303
Phone: 904/656-7884

Gay Hotline
1222 South Dale Mabry,
#608
Tampa, 33629
Phone: 813/229-8839

Compass
5405 South Dixie Highway
West Palm Beach, 33405
Phone: 407/547-2622

Georgia
Athens Gay & Lesbian Assn.
PO Box 2133
Athens, 30612
Phone: 404/548-0580

Atlanta Gay Center
63 12th Street
Atlanta, 30309
Phone: 404/876-5372
Helpline: 404/892-0661
TDD: 404/892-0661

Hawaii
Gay Information Service
Honolulu, 96837
Phone: 808/926-1000

Gay Community Center
1820 University Avenue,
2nd Floor
Honolulu, 96801
Phone: 808/951-7000

Gay/Lesbian/Bisexual
Information Line
Kahului, 96732
Phone: 808/575-2681

Idaho
The Community Center
Boise, 83701
Phone: 208/336-3870

Illinois
Gerber/Hart Library &
Archives
3352 North Paulina Street
Chicago, 60657
Phone: 312/883-3003

Horizons Community
Services
961 West Montana
Chicago, 60614
Phone: 312/472-6469
Helpline: 312/929-HELP
TDD: 312/327-HELP

In Touch Hotline
University of Illinois at
Chicago
Chicago, 60680
Phone: 312/996-5535

Rodde Center
4753 North Broadway
#1200
Chicago, 60640
Phone: 312/271-4155

Midwest Men's Center
Chicago, 60690
Phone: 312/604-4410

Kinheart Women's Center
2214 Ridge Avenue
Evanston, 60201
Phone: 708/491-1103

West Suburban Gay Assn.
Glen Ellyn, 60138
Hotline: 708/790-9742

PRIDE Youth
North Shore Youth Health
Service
1779 Maple Street
Northfield, 60093
Phone: 708/441-9880

Lesbian, Gay & Bisexual
Switchboard
c/o PLGBC
284 Illini Union
1401 West Green Street
Urbana, 61801
Phone: 217/384-8040

Indiana
Gay & Lesbian Switchboard
Rm. 48-G
Indiana Memorial Union
Bloomington, 47405
Phone: 812/855-5OUT

Gay/Lesbian Helpline
Fort Wayne
Phone: 219/744-1199

Gay/Lesbian Switchboard
Indianapolis, 46206
Phone: 317/253-GAYS

Indianapolis Youth Group
PO Box 20716
Indianapolis, 46220
Phone: 317/541-8726
Helpline: 800/347-TEEN

Iowa
Gays, Lesbians, Bisexuals
of Ames
Ames, 50010
Phone: 515/292-7000

Gay & Lesbian Information
Line
Ames, 50010
Phone: 512/294-2104

Gay & Lesbian Resource
Center
4211 Grand Avenue
Des Moines, 50312
Phone: 512/279-2110
Info. Line: 512/277-1454

Young Women's Resource Ctr.
554 28th Street
Des Moines, 50312
Phone: 515/244-4901

Gay Line
(University of Iowa)
Iowa City, 52242
Phone: 319/353-3877

United Action for Youth
410 Iowa Avenue
Iowa City, 52240
Helpline: 319/338-0059
Also: 800/850-3051 (SE IA)

Kansas

Gay & Lesbian Services
Box 13
Kansas Union
University of Kansas
Lawrence, 66045
Phone: 913/864-3091

Gay Rap Telephone Line
Topeka, 66601
Phone: 913/233-6558

Wichita Gay Information Line
Wichita, 67216
Phone: 316/269-0913

Kentucky

Gay/Lesbian Services
Lexington, 40575
Phone: 606/231-0335

Gay & Lesbian Hotline
Louisville, 40201
Phone: 502/454-6699

Louisiana

St. Louis Community Center
1022 Barracks Street
New Orleans, 70116
Phone: 504/524-7023

Le Beau Monde
PO Box 3036
Pineville, 71361
Phone: 318/442-3747

Maine

Outright
PO Box 802
Auburn, 04212
Phone: 207/783-2557

Gay/Lesbian
Community Network
PO Box 212
Bangor, 04401

Gay/Lesbian Phone Line
c/o Box 990
Caribou, 04736
Phone: 207/498-2088

Gay/Lesbian Alliance
88 Winslow Street
The Powers House
Portland, 04103
Phone: 207/874-6596

Maryland

Gay/Lesbian Community
Center
241 West Chase Street
Baltimore, 21201
Phone: 410/837-8888
TDD: 410/837-8529

Black Gay Community Ctr.
c/o 614 West Lexington
Street
Baltimore, 21201
Phone: 410/539-0942

Baltimore Gay Alliance
1504 East Baltimore Street
Baltimore, 21231
Phone: 410/276-8468

Upper County G/L Assn.
15106-A Frederick Road,
#154
Rockville, 20850
Phone: 301/340-6241

Takoma Park Lesbians & Gays
PO Box 5243
Takoma Park, 20913
Phone: 301/891-DYKE

Massachusetts
Alliance of G/L Youth
Boston
Hotline: 800/42-BAGLY

Gay & Lesbian Community Ctr.
338 Newbury Street
Boston, 02115
Phone: 617/247-2927

Gay & Lesbian Helpline
Boston
Phone: 617/267-9001

South Shore Gay/Lesbian
Alliance
PO Box 712
Bridgewater, 02324
Phone: 508/293-5183

Gay & Lesbian Alliance
PO Box 329
Dorchester, 02122
Phone: 617/825-3737

Merrimack Valley L/G
Support
Line
Lowell, 01854
Phone: 508/452-3679

North Shore Gay/Lesbian
Alliance
Box 806
Marblehead, 01945
Phone: 617/745-3848

Valley Gay Alliance
Northampton, 01061
Phone: 413/731-5403

Gay & Lesbian Alliance
PO Box 78
Yarmouth Port, 02675
Phone: 508/362-2494

Michigan
Gay Hotline
3116-18 Michigan Union
530 South State Street
Ann Arbor, 48109
Phone: 313/662-1977

PRISM
Gateway Community Services
910 Abbott Road, Suite 100
East Lansing, 48823
Phone: 517/351-4000
Statewide: 800/292-4517

Affirmations
Lesbian & Gay Community
Center
195 W. 9 Mile Rd., Suite 110
Ferndale, 48220
Phone: 313/398-4297

Detroit Area G/L Council
PO Box 20285
Ferndale, 48220
Phone: 313/837-8472

Lesbian & Gay Community
Network
909 Cherry Street, S.E.
Grand Rapids, 49506
Phone: 616/241-GAYS

Gay/Lesbian Resource
Center
Kalamazoo, 49005
Phone: 616/345-7878

Lesbian/Gay Hotline
Lansing
Phone: 517/332-3200

Minnesota
Gay, Lesbian & Bisexual
Activities
PO Box 3511
Mankato, 56002
Phone: 507/345-7799

District 202
2524 Nicollet Avenue, S.
Minneapolis, 55404
Phone: 612/871-5559

G/L Community Action
Council
Minneapolis/St. Paul
Hotline: 612/822-8661

Mississippi
Gay & Lesbian Alliance
Phone: 601/353-7611
Statewide: 800/537-0851

Missouri
Gay & Lesbian Helpline
Columbia
Phone: 314/449-4477

Gay Services Network
Gay Talk Helpline
Kansas City, 64111
Phone: 816/931-4470

Montana
Out in Montana
PO Box 8661
Missoula, 59807

Nebraska
A.N.G.L.E.
Omaha, 68131
Phone: 402/339-9948

Nevada
SNAP
Las Vegas, 89170
Phone: 702/798-9455

Gay Switchboard
MCC
1119 South Main Street
Las Vegas, 89104
Phone: 702/733-9990

New Hampshire
Network North
Madison, 03849
Phone: 603/367-8304

Gay Info. Line
Box 3148
Nashua, 03061
Phone: 603/595-2650

New Jersey
Gay Activists of NJ
South Hackensack, 07606
Helpline: 201/692-1794

Organization for
Gay Awareness
Montclair, 07042
Phone: 201/743-5322

Womyn's Network
Morristown, 07961
Helpline: 201/285-1595

Lesbian & Gay Coalition
PO Box 1431
New Brunswick, 08903
Phone: 201/763-0668

Rutgers University
Peer Counseling
New Brunswick, 08903
Phone: 908/932-7886

New Mexico
Common Bond
Albuquerque, 87125
Info. Line: 505/266-8041

Outreach
PO Box 682
Albuquerque, 87103
Phone: 505/256-4316

New York
Lesbian/Gay Community
Ctr.
PO Box 131
Albany, 12201
Phone: 518/462-6138

The S.P.A.C.E.
213 State Street
Binghamton, 13902
Phone: 607/724-2582
Eventline: 607/724-3462

G/L Community Network
2316 Delaware #267
Buffalo, 14216
Phone: 716/883-4750

The Long Island Center
Unitarian Universalist
223 Stewart Street
Garden City, 11530
Phone: 516/379-9017

Saratoga Gay Coalition
Glens Falls, 12801
Phone: 518/798-3304

Gay & Lesbian Alliance
PO Box 3785
Kingston, 12401
Phone: 914/626-3203

Youth Environmental
Services
30 Broadway
Massapequa, 11758
Phone: 516/799-3203

Lesbian & Gay Community
Services Center
208 West 13th Street
New York, 10011
Phone: 212/620-7310

Gay/Lesbian Switchboard of
New York
Phone: 212/777-1800

Hetrick-Martin Institute
401 West Street
New York, 10014
Phone: 212/633-8020

HOTT
(Health Outreach to Teens)
208 West Street
New York, 10011
Phone: 212/255-1673

Lesbian Switchboard of
New York
Phone: 212/741-2610

Reachout
Potsdam, 13676
Phone: 315/265-2422

Gay Alliance of
Genessee Valley
179 Atlantic Avenue
Rochester, 14607
Phone: 716/244-8640

Lesbian & Gay Youth of
Rochester
179 Atlantic Avenue
Rochester, 14607
Phone: 716/251-9604
Alt. Phone: 716/244-8640

Gay & Lesbian Alliance
826 Euclid Avenue
Syracuse, 13210
Phone: 315/422-5732

The Loft
255 Grove Street
White Planes, 10601
Phone: 914/948-4922

North Carolina
CLOSER
PO Box 2911
Asheville, 28802
Phone: 704/277-7815

SALGA
Asheville, 28802
Phone: 704/626-2271

Gay & Lesbian Info. Line
Asheville, 28802
Phone: 704/253-2971

Metrolina Community
Service Project
PO Box 11144
Charlotte, 28220
Phone: 704/535-6277

Stand Out Youth Alliance
PO Box 53751
Fayetteville, 28305
Phone: 910/487-6535
E-mail: standout@aol.com

Out Greensboro
c/o White Rabbit Books
1833 Spring Garden Street
Greensboro, 27403
Phone: 919/272-7604

Gay & Lesbian Helpline of
Wade County
Raleigh, 27606
Phone: 919/821-0055

Gay & Lesbian Hotline
Winston-Salem
Phone: 919/722-4040

North Dakota
Prairie Lesbian & Gay
Community
PO Box 83
Moorhead, MN 56560
Phone: 701/237-0556

Ohio
Gay/Lesbian Center
PO Box 19158
Cincinati, 45219
Phone: 513/471-8367

L/G Community Center
1418 West 29th
Cleveland, 44101
Hotline. 216/781-6736

Stonewall Community
Center
47 West 5th Avenue
Columbus, 43201
Hotline: 614/299-7764

Gay & Lesbian Hotline
Dayton, 45401
Phone: 513/228-4875

TGALA
PO Box 4642
Old West End Station
Toledo, 43610
Phone: 419/243-9351

Oklahoma
Oasis Community Center
2135 NW 39th Street
Oklahoma City, 73112
Phone: 405/525-2437

TOHR Gay/Lesbian
Helpline
Tulsa, 74152
Phone: 918/743-GAYS

Oregon
The Other Side
PO Box 5672
Bend, 97708
Hotline: 503/388-2395

Gay & Lesbian Outreach
Box 4212
Coos Bay, 97420
Hotline: 503/269-4183

Gay & Lesbian Alliance
Eugene, 97403
Phone: 503/686-3360

Gay & Lesbian Helpline
Eugene, 97405
Phone: 503/683-CHAT

Phoenix Rising
620 SW 5th Avenue
Portland, 97204
Phone: 503/223-8299

Gay & Lesbian Community
Ctr.
3856 Carnes Road
Roseburg, 97470
Phone: 503/672-4126

Pennsylvania
Justice Campaign
PO Box 614
Harrisburg, 17108
Phone: 717/234-2250

Gay & Lesbian Switchboard
Harrisburg, 17108
Phone: 717/234-0328

Gay/Lesbian Helpline
Lancaster, 17603
Phone: 717/397-0691

Gay Switchboard
Philadelphia
Phone: 215/546-7100

Penguin Place
G/L Community Center
201 South Camac Street
Philadelphia, 19107
Phone: 215/732-2220

Lesbian Hotline
Philadelphia, 19104
Phone: 215/222-5110

Gay & Lesbian Community
Ctr.
2214 East Carson Street
Pittsburgh, 15206
Phone: 412/431-LGCC

Gay & Lesbian Switchboard
State College, 16804
Phone: 814/237-1950

Susquehanna Lambda
PO Box 2510
Williamsport, 17703
Phone: 717/327-1411

Rhode Island
Gay/Lesbian Helpline
PO Box 5671
Providence, 02903
Phone: 401/751-3322

South Carolina
G/L Pride Movement
Columbia, 29211
Phone: 803/782-2912

G/L Switchboard
Palmetto G/L Association
Greenville, 29603
Phone: 803/271-4207

South Dakota
The Coalition
Sioux Falls, 57105
Phone: 605/332-4599

Tennessee
Gay Helpline
Knoxville, 37901
Phone: 615/521-6546

Memphis G/L Community
Ctr.
1291 Madison Avenue
Memphis, 38104
Phone: 901/276-4651

One in Ten Youth Services
703 Berry Road
Nashville, 37204
Phone: 615/297-0008

TGALA
PO Box 41305
Nashville, 37204
Phone: 615/292-4820

Texas
Out-Youth Austin
2330 Guadalupe Street
Austin, 78705
Phone: 512/472-9264
Helpline: 800/96-YOUTH
E-mail*: outyouth@out-
youth.austin.tx.us
*pen-pal service

G/L Community Center
Dallas Gay Alliance
PO Box 190712
Dallas, 75219
Phone: 214/528-4233

GLB Young Adults
2701 Reagan Street
Dallas, 75219
Phone: 214/521-5342
    ext. 260

LAMBDA Services
El Paso, 79931
Hotline. 915/562-4297

Lesbian/Gay Alliance
Fort Worth, 76110
Phone: 817/336-8242

G/L Switchboard
Houston, 77266
Phone: 713/529-3211

Community Outreach
Center
102 N Avenue South
Lubbock, 79464
Phone: 806/762-1019

The Resource Center
121 West Woodlawn
San Antonio, 78212
Phone: 512/732-0751

Utah
Gay/Lesbian Alliance
of Cache Valley
UMC 0100
Box 119
Tagart Student Center
Logan, 84322
Phone: 801/752-1129

Utah Stonewall Center
450 South 900 East, #140
Salt Lake City, 84100
Phone: 801/539-8800

Vermont
Coalition of Lesbians
& Gay Men
PO Box 1125
Montpelier, 05602

Outright Vermont
Burlington
Phone: 802/865-9677

Virginia
G/L Community Association
PO Box 19401
Alexandria, 22320
Phone: 703/684-0444

Kindred Spirits
Charlottesville, 22903
Phone: 804/296-7737

L/G Student Union
Helpline
Box 525
Newcomb Hall Station
Charlottesville, 22904
Phone: 804/971-4942

Shenandoah Valley Lambda
Dayton, 22821
Phone: 703/289-9025

Gay Information Line
Norfolk, 23501
Phone: 804/622-GAYS

Roanoke Valley Gay Alliance
Roanoke, 24002
Phone: 703/982-3733

FLGCA
Springfield, 22152
Phone: 703/451-9528

Washington
L/G Resource Center
CAB 305 Evergreen State
College
Olympia, 98505
Phone: 206/866-6000
        ext 6544

Stonewall Youth
PO Box 7383
Olympia, 98507
Phone: 206/705-2738

Lambert House Youth
Center
1818 15th Avenue
Seattle, 98122
Phone: 206/322-2735

Odyssey
1101 West College Avenue
Rm 401
Spokane, 99201
Phone: 509/324-1547
Helpline: 800/456-3236

Oasis Youth Association
3629 S. D St.
Tacoma, 98408
Phone: 206/591-6060
Drop-in Ctr: 206/596-2860

West Virginia
G/L Helpline
Morgantown, 26506
Phone: 304/292-GAY2

Wisconsin
G/L Alliance
1411 Ellis Avenue
Box 247A
Ashland, 54806
Phone: 715/682-1595

Madison Community
United
310 E. Wilson
Madison, 53703
Phone: 608/255-8582

Gay Information
Milwaukee, 93202
Phone: 414/444-7331

Wyoming
Gay & Lesbian Oriented
Youth
(GLORY)
PO Box 9725
Casper, 82609
Phone: 307/577-7969

United Gays & Lesbians
Laramie, 82070
Phone: 307/ 635-4301

A Different Light
489 Castro Street
San Francisco, CA 94114
Phone: 415/431-0891

A Different Light
8853 Santa Monica Blvd.
West Hollywood, CA 90069
Phone: 213/854-6601

Obelisk
1029 University Avenue
San Diego, CA 92103
Phone: 619/297-4171

Category Six Books
1029 E. 11th Avenue
Denver, CO 80218
Phone: 303/832-6263

Lambda Rising
1625 Connecticut Avenue, NW
Washington, DC 20009
Phone: 202/462-6969
E-mail:
lambdarising@his.com
Free catalog/mail order service: 800/621-6969

Lambda Rising
39 Baltimore Avenue
Rehoboth Beach, DE 19971
Phone: 302/227-6969

Outwrite Bookstore &
    Coffeeshop
931 Monroe Drive, #108
Atlanta, GA 30308
Phone: 404/607-0082

People Like Us
3321 North Clark Street
Chicago, IL 60657
Phone: 312/248-6363

Faubourg Marigny
Bookstore
600 Frenchmen
New Orleans, LA 70116
Phone: 504/943-9875

PLU Books & Gifts
PO Box 44205
Shreveport, LA 71134
Phone: 318/861-4223

Glad Day Bookshop
673 Boylston Street
Boston, MA 02116
Phone: 617/542-0144

Lambda Rising
241 West Chase Street
Baltimore, MD 21201
Phone: 301/234-0069

Sons & Daughters
PO Box 6148
Grand Rapids, MI
49516
Phone: 313/645-2210

Sons & Daughters
962 Cherry Street
Grand Rapids, MI 49506
Phone: 616/459-8877

A Brother's Touch
2327 Hennepin Avenue
Minneapolis, MN 55405
Phone: 612/377-6279

Our World Too
11 South Vandevanter Street
St. Louis, MO 63108
Phone: 314/533-5322

White Rabbit Books
1833 Spring Garden Street
Greensboro, NC 27403
Phone: 919/272-7604

White Rabbit Books
309 West Martin Street
Raleigh, NC 27603
Phone: 919/856-1429

A Different Light
151 West 19th Street
New York, NY 10011
Phone: 212/989-4850

Oscar Wilde Memorial
Bookshop
15 Christopher Street
New York, NY 10014
Phone: 212/255-8097

Giovanni's Room
345 South 12th Street
Philadelphia, PA 19107
Phone: 215/923-2960

Crossroads Books
3930 Cedar Springs
Dallas, TX 75219
Phone: 214/521-8919

Liberty Books
1014-B North Lamar
Austin, TX 78703
Phone: 512/495-9737

Out Right Books
#110
485 South Independence
Blvd.
Virginia Beach, VA 23452
Phone: 804/490-6658

Phoenix Rising
19 North Belmont Avenue
Richmond, VA 23221
Phone: 804/355-7939

Beyond the Closet
Bookstore
1501 Belmont Avenue
Seattle, WA 98122
Phone: 206/322-4609

Glad Day Bookshop
598 Yonge Street
Toronto, Ont. M4Y 1Z3
Canada
Phone: 416/961-4161

L'Androgyne
3636 Boulevard St. Laurent
Montreal, Quebec H2X 2V4
Canada
Phone: 514/542-4765

Little Sisters
1221 Thurlow Street
Vancouver, BC V6E 1X4
Canada
Phone: 604/669-1753

RELIGIOUS ORGANIZATIONS

Affirm (United Church of
Canada)
PO Box 62
Station H
Toronto, Ontario M4C 5H7
Canada

Affirmation (Mormon)
213/255-7251

Affirmation (Methodist)
708/475-0499

American Baptists
Concerned
415/465-8652

Dignity (Catholic)
800/877-8797

Integrity (Episcopal)
201/868-2485

First Unitarian Church
(Unitarian Universalist)
4190 Front Street
San Diego, 92103
619/298-9978

UNIVERSAL FELLOWSHIP OF METROPOLITAN COMMUNITY CHURCHES

AUSTRALIA
New South Wales
MCC Northern Rivers
PO Box 6069
South Lismore, 2480
06/689-5105

MCC of the Good Shepherd
15 Francis Street
Sydney
02/638-3298

Victoria
MCC Melbourne
325 Dorcas Street
S. Melbourne
03/528-5381

CANADA
Alberta
Alleluia MCC
#301, 223 - 12th Avenue, SW
Calgary, T2R 0G9
403/264-0320

MCC Calgary
204 16th Avenue, NW
Calgary, T2M 0H4
403/277-4004

British Columbia
Christ Alive MCC
3214 West 10th Avenue
Vancouver, V6B 4B2
604/739-7959

Manitoba
MCC Winnipeg
St. Stephen's
Broadway & Kennedy
Winnipeg, R3C 4K9
204/001-2219

Nova Scotia
Safe Harbour MCC
2107 Brunswick Street
Halifax, B3K 5T9
902/454-2522

Ontario
Gentle Spirit MCC
82 Sydemham Street
Kingston, K7L 4Y8
613/547-2107

MCC Ottawa ECM
320 Elgin Street
Ottawa, K1G 5K9
613/232-0241

Christos MCC
353 Shelbourne Street
Toronto, M5A 2S3
416/925-7924

UNITED STATES
Alabama
Covenant MCC
3001 4th Avenue, South
Birmingham, 35210
205/326-8529

MCC of Huntsville
#102
2400 Bob Wallace
Huntsville, 35801
205/533-6220

Alaska
Lamb of God MCC
#4
615 Hollywood Drive
Anchorage, 99514
907/258-5266

Arizona
Gentle Shepherd MCC
3425 East Mountain View
Phoenix, 85028
602/996-7644

Arkansas
MCC of the Living Spring
17 Elk Street
Eureka Springs, 72632
501/253-9337

California
MCC of the Harvest
2415 Alta Vista Drive
Bakersfield, 93385
805/327-3724

MCC of the Vineyard
106 East Shields
Fresno
209/224-3871

MCC in the Valley
5730 Cahuenga Boulevard
North Hollywood, 91601
818/762-1133

MCC San Diego
4333 30th Street
San Diego, 92104
619/280-4333

MCC Ventura
1848 Poli Street
Ventura, 93002
805/643-0502

Colorado
Pikes Peak MCC
730 North. Tejon Street
Colorado Springs
719/634-3771

Florida
Sunshine Cathedral
330 SW 27th Street
Ft. Lauderdale
305/462-2004

St. John the Apostle
2209 Unity Avenue
Ft. Myers, 33902
813/433-1007

Georgia
MCC Savannah
321 East York Street
Savannah, 31416
912/925-3731

Indiana
Tri State MCC
2910 East Morgan Avenue
Evansville, 47732
812/429-3512

Iowa
MCC of Sioux City
2405 Jackson Street
Sioux City, 51102
712/258-3116

Kansas
MCC Topeka
2425 SE Indiana
Topeka, 66604
913/271-8431

Montana
Family of God MCC
645 Howard
Billings, 59104
406/245-7066

Shepherd of the Plains
1505 17th Avenue SW
Great Falls
406/771-1070

New Hampshire
MCC in the Mountain
Church of Christ at
Dartmouth College
Hanover, 03755
603/298-5451

New Mexico
Emmanuel MCC
201 Dallas NE
Albuquerque
505/268-0599

New York
MCC New York
446 West 36th Street
New York, 10018
212/629-7440

Ray of Hope
138 West Beard Avenue
Syracuse, 13217
518/762-8397

Oklahoma
Family of Faith
500 West A Street
Jenks, 74037
918/298-4622

Lighthouse MCC
3629 NW 19th Street
OK City, 73126
405/942-2822

Oregon
MCC Portland
NE 24th & Broadway
Portland, 97232
503/281-8868

Sweet Spirit MCC
1410 12th Street S.
Salem, 97309
503/363 6618

Texas
Cathedral of Hope
5910 Cedar Springs
Dallas, 75235
214/351-6099

MCC San Antonio
1136 West Woodlawn
San Antonio
210/734-0048

Utah
Sacred Light of Christ
823 South 600 E.
Salt Lake City
801/595-0052

OVER THE INTERNET

BiNet USA:
rain@glib.org

Gay & Lesbian Association
of Nova Scotia:
daniel@nstn.ns.ca

Gay & Lesbian Young
Adults of Dallas:
shishkabob@aol.com

The International Lesbian
& Gay Youth Organization:
PO Box 42463
Washington, DC 20015
ay361@freenet.toronto.on.
ca

!OutProud!
The National Coalition for
Gay, Lesbian & Bisexual
Youth:
glbyouth@aol.com

Parents, Families and
Friends of Lesbians and
Gays (P-FLAG):
Suite 1030
1101-14th Street, NW
Washington, DC 20005
pflagntl@aol.com

California
ONE Institute Library
(Housed at USC)
746 West Adams
Los Angeles

Lesbian & Gay Historical
Society
4545 Park Boulevard
San Diego, 92103
619/260-1522

Gay & Lesbian Historical
Society
2940 16th Street
PO Box 424280
San Francisco, 94142
415/626-0980

June Mazer Lesbian
Collection
626 North Robertson
Boulevard
West Hollywood, 90069
310/659-2478

Florida
Stonewall Library &
Archives
c/o Holy Spirit MCC
330 S.W. 27th Street
Fort Lauderdale, 33315
305/462-2004

Illinois
Gerbert/Hart Library &
Archives
3352 North Paulina Street
Chicago, 60657
312/883-3003

Massachusetts
Women's Movement
Archives & Library
46 Pleasant Street
Cambridge, 02139
617/354-8807

Minnesota
Quatrefoil Library
1619 Dayton Avenue
St. Paul, 55104
612/641-0969

New York
National Museum of
Lesbian and Gay History
208 West 13th Street
New York, 10011
212/620-7310

Parker/Russo Center
208 West 13th Street
New York, 10011
212/966-8400

Pennsylvania
Lesbian & Gay
Library/Archives
201 South Camac Street
Philadelphia, 19107
215/732-2220

Texas

Dallas Gay/Lesbian Historic
Archives
6146 St. Moritz
Dallas, 75214
214/021-1633

Metropolitan
Community
Church Library
1919 Decatur
Houston, 77007
214/821-1653

INTRODUCTION

1. Gerald Unks, "Thinking About the Homosexual Adolescent," *The High School Journal* (Chapel Hill, North Carolina: The University of North Carolina Press, 1994), Vol. 77, Nos. 1 & 2; Gerald Unks, editor; p. 1.

CHAPTER 1

1. Unks, p. 4.
2. Gilbert Herdt & Andrew Boxer, *Children of Horizons* (Boston: Beacon Press, 1993), p. 175.
3. Dennis A. Anderson, M.D., "Lesbian and Gay Adolescents: Social and Developmental Considerations," *The High School Journal*, p. 14.
4. Gilbert Herdt, "Introduction: Gay and Lesbian Youth, Emergent Identities, and Cultural Scenes at Home and Abroad," *Gay and Lesbian Youth* (New York: Harrington Park Press, 1989); Gilbert Herdt, editor; p. 116.
5. Debra Boyer, Ph.D., "Male Prostitution and Homosexual Identity," *Gay and Lesbian Youth*, p. 167.
6. Warren J. Blumenfeld, "'Gay/Straight' Alliances: Transforming Pain into Pride," *The High School Journal*, p. 117.

7. Andi O'Conor, "Who Gets Called Queer in School? Lesbians, Gay and Bisexual Teenagers, Homophobia and High School," *The High School Journal,* p. 7.

8. Anderson, p. 14.

9. *Children of Horizons,* p. 21.

10. Bob Tremble, Margret Schneider, and Carol Appathurai, "Growing Up Gay or Lesbian in a Multicultural Context," *Gay and Lesbian Youth,* p. 261.

11. Brian McNaught, *Gay Issues in the Workplace* (New York: St. Martin's Press, 1993), pp. 14-15.

12. Blumenfeld, pp. 117-118. Also, "From Silence to Suicide," by B. Jaye Miller in *Homophobia: How We All Pay the Price* (Boston: Beacon Press, 1992), pp. 79-94; Warren J. Blumenfeld, editor; and "Gay Youth: An Educational Video for the Nineties" (New Almaden, California: Wolfe Video) produced by Pam Walton.

13. *Children of Horizons,* p. 109.

CHAPTER 2

1. *Children of Horizons,* p. 100.

2. Ibid., p. 197.

3. Richard R. Troiden, Ph.D., "The Formation of Homosexual Identities," *Gay and Lesbian Youth,* pp. 55-57.

4. Aaron Fricke, *Reflections of a Rock Lobster* (Boston: Alyson Publications, 1981), p. 44.

5. Mel White, *Stranger at the Gate* (New York: Simon and Schuster, 1994), p. 160.

6. *Children of Horizons,* p. 18.

7. Ibid., p. 4.

8. Ibid., p. 105.

9. O'Conor, p. 10.

10. *Children of Horizons,* p. 217.

11. Ibid., p. 210.

12. Ibid., p. 2.

13. Steve Silberman, "We're Teen, We're Queer, and We've Got E-mail," *Wired,* November, 1994, p. 76.

14. "Contemplations of the First Year Out," ©Trey Harris, used with permission of the author.

CHAPTER 3

1. Children of Horizons, p. 222.
2. Virginia Uribe, Ph.D., "Project 10: A School-Based Outreach to Gay and Lesbian Youth," The High School Journal, p. 108.
3. Margaret Schneider, Ph.D., "Sappho Was a Right-On Adolescent: Growing Up Lesbian," Gay and Lesbian Youth, p. 117.
4. "Making Schools Safe for Gay and Lesbian Youth: Breaking the Silence in Schools and in Families" (Boston: The Governor's Commission of Gay and Lesbian Youth; February 25, 1993), p. 9. Also, O'Conor, p. 11.
5. Unks, p. 2.
6. "Making Schools Safe for Gay and Lesbian Youth: Breaking the Silence in Schools and in Families," p. 9.
7. Alfred P. Kielwasser and Michelle A. Wolf, "Silence, Difference, and Annihilation: Understanding the Impact of Mediated Heterosexism on High School Students," The High School Journal, p. 69.
8. Ibid., p. 61.
9. Children of Horizons, p. 223.
10. Kielwasser and Wolf, p. 71.
11. "Mom Banned from Son's School," Associated Press, San Diego Union-Tribune, December 4, 1994, p. A-3.
12. Unks, p. 3.
13. Children of Horizons, p. 226.
14. Uribe, p. 112.
15. Kit R. Roane, "Two White Sport Coats, Two Pink Carnations: One Couple for a Prom," New York Times, May 22, 1994.
16. "Action Items to Make Schools Safe for Gay Youth" (Boston: The Governor's Commission of Gay and Lesbian Youth), p. 1.
17. Faye Penn, "Whose Children Are They Anyway?" QW, September 20, 1992, p. 23.
18. Sean Hilditch, "Over the Rainbow: Mary Cummins Is No Judy Garland," QW, September 20, 1993, p. 25.
19. Sarah J. Rivera, "Austin Schools' Code of Conduct to Add Protection for Gays, Lesbians," Daily Texan, November 8, 1994.

20. Arthur Lipkin, "The Case for a Gay and Lesbian Curriculum," *The High School Journal,* p. 98.

CHAPTER 4

1. John J. McNeill, *The Church and the Homosexual* (Boston: Beacon Press, 1900), p. 36.
2. McNaught, p. 97.
3. McNeill, p. 37.
4. White, p. 38.
5. Ibid., pp. 273-274.
6. McNeill, p. 57; White, p. 237.
7. White, p. 238.
8. Ibid., p. 240.
9. McNaught, p. 34.
10. *Children of Horizons,* p. 60.
11. Keith Clark, "Young Gays Engaging in Risky Sex; High HIV Infection Reported," *Gay & Lesbian Times,* December 23, 1993, p. 15.
12. Douglas A. Feldman, Ph.D., "Gay Youth and AIDS," *Gay and Lesbian Youth,* p. 187.
13. David Gelman, et al., "The Young and the Reckless," *Newsweek,* January 11, 1993, p. 60.
14. Clark, p. 15.
15. Michelangelo Signorile, "Unsafe Like Me," *Out,* October, 1994, p. 24.
16. Kielwasser and Wolf, p. 58.

reading of special interest
to young people

Nonfiction

Alyson, Sasha, ed. *Young, Gay, and Proud!*. Boston: Alyson Publications, 1980.

Bell, Ruth, et. al. *Changing Bodies, Changing Lives: A Book for Teens on Sex and Relationships.* New York: Random House, 1988.

Borhek, Mary V. *Coming Out to Parents.* Cleveland, Ohio: Pilgrim Press, 1983.

Clark, Don. *The New Loving Someone Gay.* Berkeley, California: Celestial Arts, 1987.

Cohen, Susan, and Daniel Cohen. *When Someone You Know is Gay.* New York: M. Evans, 1989.

Dew, Robb Forman. *The Family Heart: A Memoir of When Our Son Came Out.* Reading, Massachusetts: Addison-Wesley Publishing Co., 1994.

Eichberg, Rob. *Coming Out, an Act of Love.* New York: Plume, 1991.

Fricke, Aaron. *Reflections of a Rock Lobster.* Boston: Alyson Publications, 1981.

Fricke, Aaron. *Sudden Strangers.* New York: St. Martin's Press, 1991.

Heron, Ann, ed. *One Teenager in Ten.* Boston: Alyson Publications, 1983.

Heron, Ann, ed. *Two Teenagers in Twenty.* Boston: Alyson Publications, 1994.

Jackson-Paris, Rod and Bob. *Straight From the Heart: A Love Story.* New York: Warner Books, 1994.

Marcus, Eric. *Is It a Choice?* New York: HarperCollins Publishers, 1993.

McNaught, Brian. *On Being Gay.* New York: St. Martin's Press, 1988.

Rench, Janice E. *Understanding Sexual Identity.* Minneapolis: Lerner Publications, 1990.

White, Mel. *Stranger at the Gate.* New York: Simon & Schuster, 1994.

Fiction

Bauer, Marion Dane. *Am I Blue? Coming Out From the Silence.* New York: HarperCollins Publishers, 1994.

Brown, Rita Mae. *Rubyfruit Jungle.* New York: Bantam Books, 1977.

Garden, Nancy. *Annie on My Mind.* New York: Farrar, Straus and Giroux, 1982.

Greene, Bette. *The Drowning of Stephan Jones.* New York: Bantam Books, 1991.

Kerr, M.E. *Deliver Us From Evie.* New York: HarperCollins Publishers, 1994.

Leavitt, David. *The Lost Language of Cranes.* New York: Bantam Books, 1986.

Salat, Cristina. *Living in Secret.* New York: Bantam Books, 1993.

van Dijk, Lutz. Translated by E. Crawford. *Damned Strong Love: The True Story of Willi G. and Stephan K.* New York: Holt/Edge, 1995.

Warren, Patricia Nell. *The Front Runner.* New York: Bantam Books, 1975.

    Harlan's Race. Beverly Hills, California: Wildcat Press, 1994.

bibliography

Alyson, Sasha, ed. *Young, Gay, and Proud!* Boston: Alyson Publications, 1991.

Associated Press. "Mom is Banned from Son's School," *San Diego Union-Tribune,* December 4, 1994.

Bauer, Marion Dane, ed. *Am I Blue? Coming Out from the Silence.* New York: HarperCollins Publishers, 1994.

Boswell, John. *Christianity, Social Tolerance, and Homosexuality.* Chicago: University of Chicago Press, 1980.

Boyd, Malcolm. *Gay Priest: An Inner Journey.* New York: St. Martin's Press, 1986.

Blumenfeld, Warren J., ed. *Homophobia: How We All Pay the Price.* Boston: Beacon Press, 1992.

Clark, Keith. "Young Gays Engaging in Risky Sex; High HIV Infection Reported," *Gay & Lesbian Times,* December 23, 1993.

Drake, David. *The Night Larry Kramer Kissed Me.* New York: Anchor Books, 1994.

Dew, Robb Forman. *The Family Heart: A Memoir of When Our Son Came Out.* Reading, MA: Addison-Wesley Publishing Co., 1994.

Fricke, Aaron. *Reflections of a Rock Lobster.* Boston: Alyson Publications, 1981.

Fricke, Aaron, and Walter Fricke. *Sudden Strangers: The Story of a Gay Son and His Father.* New York: St. Martin's Press, 1991.

"Gay and Lesbian Teens" (video) on *Soap Box with Tom Cottle,* PBS Video (WGBY-TV), 1993.

Gelman, David, et al. "The Young and the Reckless," *Newsweek,* January 11, 1993.

Governor's Commission for Gay Youth. "Action Items to Make Schools Safe for Gay Youth." Boston.

Governor's Commission for Gay Youth. "Making Schools Safe for Gay and Lesbian Youth: Breaking the Silence in Schools and in Families." Boston: February 25, 1993.

Henry, William A., III. "Pride and Prejudice," Time, June 27, 1994.

Herdt, Gilbert, and Andrew Boxer. *Children of Horizons.* Boston: Beacon Press, 1993.

Herdt, Gilbert, ed. *Gay and Lesbian Youth.* New York: Harrington Park Press, 1989.

Heron, Ann, ed. *One Teenager in Ten.* Boston: Alyson Publications, 1983.

Heron, Ann, ed. *Two Teenagers in Twenty.* Boston: Alyson Publications, 1994.

Hilditch, Sean. "Over the Rainbow: Mary Cummins Is No Judy Garland," *QW,* September 20, 1992.

Hutchins, Loraine and Lani Kaahumanu. *Bi Any Other Name:* Bisexual People Speak Out. Boston: Alyson Publications, 1990.

Kerr, M.E. *Deliver Us from Evie.* New York: HarperCollins Publishers, 1994.

Leavitt, David. *The Lost Language of Cranes.* New York: Bantam Books, 1986.

Marcus, Eric. *Is It a Choice?* New York: HarperCollins Publishers, 1993.

Massachusetts Department of Education. "Gay and Lesbian Youth Making History in Massachusetts" (video). Boston: Governor's Commission on Gay Youth, 1994.

McCann, Harry. "GLAAD Wants to Show Roger an Open Door," *Update,* July 27, 1994.

McNaught, Brian. *Gay Issues in the Workplace.* New York: St. Martin's Press, 1993.

McNaught, Brian. *On Being Gay*. New York: St. Martin's Press, 1988.

McNeill, John J *The Church and the Homosexual*. Boston: Beacon Press, 1988.

Moyers, Bill. "The New Holy War," *Bill Moyers' Journal*. New York: Public Affairs Television, Inc., WNET, 1993.

Ocamb, Karen. "Rev. Sheldon Goes to Washington," *Gay & Lesbian Times,* December 29, 1995.

Penn, Faye. "Whose Children Are They Anyway?," *QW,* September 20, 1992.

Planck, Corri. "Roseanne Named 'Advocate's' Person of the Year," *Gay & Lesbian Times,* December 29, 1994.

Plant, Richard. *The Pink Triangle: The Nazi War Against Homosexuals*. New York: Owl Books, 1986.

Rivera, Sarah J. "Austin Schools' Code of Conduct to Add Protection for Gays, Lesbians," *Daily Texan,* November 8, 1994.

Roane, Kit R. "Two White Sport Coats, Two Pink Carnations: One Couple for a Prom," *New York Times,* May 22, 1994.

Russo, Vito. *The Celluloid Closet*. New York: Harper & Row, 1987.

Rutledge, Leigh W. *Unnatural Quotations*. Boston: Alyson Publications, 1988.

Signorile, Michelangelo. "Unsafe Like Me," *Out,* October, 1994.

Silberman, Steve. "We're Teen, We're Queer, and We've Got E-mail," *Wired,* November, 1994.

Spong, John Shelby. *Rescuing the Bible from Fundamentalism*. New York: HarperCollins, 1992.

"Tiny Church Starts Big Controversy," *San Diego Union-Tribune,* December 25, 1994.

Unks, Gerald, ed. *The High School Journal*. Vol. 77, Nos. 1 & 2 Chapel Hill, NC: The University of North Carolina Press, 1994.

Walton, Pam, producer. "Gay Youth: An Educational Video for the Nineties." New Almaden, CA: Wolfe Video.

White, Mel. *Stranger at the Gate*. New York: Simon & Schuster, 1994.

index